Modern Spiritualism

Uriah Smith

Chapter One.

Opening Thought.

What think ye? Whence is it—from heaven or of men? Such was the nature of the question addressed by our Saviour to the men of his time, concerning the baptism of John. It is the crucial question by which to test every system that comes to us in the garb of religion: Is it from heaven or of men? And if a true answer to the question can be found, it must determine our attitude toward it; for if it is from heaven, it challenges at once our acceptance and profound regard, but if it is of men, sooner or later, in this world or in the world to come, it will be destroyed with all its followers; for our Saviour has declared that every plant which our heavenly Father has not planted shall be rooted up. Matt. 15:13.

To those who do not believe in any "heavenly Father," nor in "Christ the Saviour," nor in any "revealed word of God," we would say that these points will be assumed in this work rather than [pg 010] directly argued, though many incidental proofs will appear, to which we trust our friends will be pleased to give some consideration. But we address ourselves particularly to those who still have faith in God the Father of all; in his divine Son, our Lord Jesus Christ, through whose blood we have redemption; in the Bible as the inspired revelation of God's will; and in the Holy Spirit as the enlightener of the mind, and the sanctifier of the soul. To all those to whom this position is common ground, the Bible will be the standard of authority, and the court of last appeal, in the study upon which we now enter.

A Manifestation of Power.

Spiritualism cannot be disposed of with a sneer. A toss of the head and a cry of "humbug," will not suffice to meet its claims and the testimony of careful, conservative men who have studied thoroughly into the genuineness of its manifestations, and have sought for the secret of its power, and have become satisfied as to the one, and been wholly baffled as to the other. That there have been abundant instances of attempted fraud, deception, jugglery, and imposition, is not to be denied. But this does not by any means set aside the fact that there have been manifestations of more than human power, the evidence for which has never been impeached. The detection of a few sham mediums, who are trying to impose upon the credulity of the public, for money, may satisfy the careless and unthinking, that the whole affair is a humbug. Such will dismiss the matter [pg 011] from their minds, and depart, easier subjects to be captured by the movement when some manifestation appears for which they can find no explanation. But the more thoughtful and careful observers well know that the exposure of these mountebanks does not account for the numberless manifestations of power, and the steady current of phenomena, utterly inexplicable on any human hypothesis, which have attended the movement from the beginning.

The Philadelphia *North American*, of July 31, 1885, published a communication from Thomas R. Hazard, in which he says:—

> "But Spiritualism, whatever may be thought of it, must be recognized as a fact. It is one of the characteristic intellectual or emotional phenomena of the times, and as such, it is deserving of a more serious examination than it has yet received. There are those who say it is all humbug, and that everything outside of the ordinary course which takes place at the so-called séances, is the direct result of fraudulent and deliberative imposture; in short, that every Spiritualist must be either a fool or a knave. The serious objection to this hypothesis is that the explanation is almost as difficult of belief as the occurrences which it explains. There must certainly be some Spiritualists who are both honest and intelligent; and if the manifestations at the séances were altogether and invariably fraudulent, surely the whole thing must have collapsed long before this; and the Seybert Commission, which finds it necessary to extend its investigations over an indefinite period, which will

certainly not be less than a year, would have been able to sweep the delusion away in short order."

The phenomena are so well known, that it is unnecessary to recount them here. Among them may be mentioned such achievements as these: Various articles have been transported from place to [pg 012] place, without human hands, but by the agency of so-called spirits only; beautiful music has been produced independently of human agency, with and without the aid of visible instruments; many well-attested cases of healing have been presented; persons have been carried through the air by the spirits in the presence of many witnesses; tables have been suspended in the air with several persons upon them; purported spirits have presented themselves in bodily form and talked with an audible voice; and all this not once or twice merely, but times without number, as may be gathered from the records of Spiritualism, all through its history.

A few particular instances, as samples, it may be allowable to notice: Not many years since, Joseph Cook made his memorable tour around the world. In Europe he met the famous German philosopher, Professor Zöllner. Mr. Zöllner had been carefully investigating the phenomena of Spiritualism, and assured Mr. Cook of the following occurrences as facts, under his own observation: Knots had been found tied in the middle of cords, by some invisible agency, while both ends were made securely fast, so that they could not be tampered with; messages were written between doubly and trebly sealed slates; coin had passed through a table in a manner to illustrate the suspension of the laws of impenetrability of matter; straps of leather were knotted under his own hand; the impression of two feet was given on sooted paper pasted inside of two sealed slates; whole and uninjured wooden rings were placed [pg 013] around the standard of a card table, over either end of which they could by no possibility be slipped; and finally the table itself, a heavy beechen structure, wholly disappeared, and then fell from the top of the room where Professor Zöllner and his friends were sitting.

In further confirmation of the fact that real spiritualistic manifestations are no sleight-of-hand performances, we cite the case of Harry Kellar, a professional performer, as given in "Nineteenth Century Miracles," p. 213.

The séance was held with the medium, Eglinton, in Calcutta, India, Jan. 25, 1882. He says:—

> "It is needless to say that I went as a skeptic; but I must own that I have come away utterly unable to explain by any natural means the phenomena that I witnessed on Tuesday evening."

He then describes the particulars of the séance. An intelligence, purporting to be the spirit of one Geary, gave a communication. Mr. Kellar did not recognize the name nor recall the man. The message was repeated, with the added circumstances of the time and particulars of a previous meeting, when Mr. Kellar recalled the events, and, much to his surprise, the whole matter came clearly to his recollection. He then adds:—

> "I still remain a skeptic as regards Spiritualism, but I repeat my inability to explain or account for what must have been an intelligent force which produced the writing on the slate, which, if my senses are to be relied on, was in no way the result of trickery or sleight-of-hand."

[pg 014]
Another instance from "Home Circle," p. 25, is that of Mr. Bellachini, also a professional conjuror, of Berlin, Germany. His interview was with the celebrated medium, Mr. Slade. From his testimony we quote the following:—

> "I have not, in the smallest degree, found anything to be produced by prestidigitative manifestations or mechanical apparatus; and any explanation of the experiments which took place under the circumstances and conditions then obtaining, by any reference to prestidigitation, is *absolutely impossible*.
>
> I declare, moreover, the published opinions of laymen as to the 'How' of this subject, to be premature, and according to my views and experience, false and one-sided."—*Dated,Berlin,Dec.6,1877.*

When professional conjurors bear such testimony as this, while it does not prove Spiritualism to be what it claims to be, it does disprove the humbug theory.

In addition to this, it appears that two propositions, one of $2000, and the other of $5000, have been offered to the one who claimed to be able to duplicate all the manifestations of Spiritualism, to duplicate two well-authenticated tests; but the challenge has never been accepted, nor the reward claimed. See *Religio-Philosophical Journal,* of Jan. 15, 1881, and January, 1883.

A writer in the *Spiritual Clarion,* in an article on "The Millennium of Spiritualism," bears the following testimony in regard to the power and strength of the movement:—

> "This revelation has been with a power, a might, that if divested of its almost universal benevolence, had been a terror [pg 015] to the very soul; the hair of the very bravest had stood on end, and his chilled blood had crept back upon his heart, at the sights and sounds of its inexplicable phenomena. It comes with foretokening and warning. It has been, from the very first, its own best prophet, and step by step, it has foretold the progress it would make. It comes, too, most triumphant. No faith before it ever took such a victorious stand in its very infancy. It has swept like a hurricane of fire through the land, compelling faith from the baffled scoffer, and the most determined doubter."

Dr. W. F. Barrett, Professor of Experimental Physics in the Royal College of Dublin, says:—

> "It is well known to those who have made the phenomena of Spiritualism the subject of prolonged and careful inquiry, in the spirit of exact and unimpassioned scientific research, that beneath a repellent mass of imposture and delusion there remain certain inexplicable and startling facts which science can neither explain away nor deny."—*"Automatic, or Spirit, Writing," p.11(1896).*

In the *Arena* of November, 1892, p. 688, Mr. M. J. Savage, the noted Unitarian minister of Boston, says:—

> "Next comes what are ordinarily classed together as 'mediumistic phenomena.' The most important of these are psychometry, 'vision' of 'spirit' forms, claimed communications by means of rappings, table

> movements, automatic writing, independent writing, trance speaking, etc. With them also ought to be noted what are generally called physical phenomena, though in most cases, since they are intelligibly directed, the use of the word 'physical,' without this qualification, might be misleading. These physical phenomena include such facts as the movement of material objects by other than the ordinary muscular force, the making objects heavier or lighter when tested by the scales, the playing on musical instruments by some invisible power, etc.... Now all of these referred to (with the exception of independent writing, and materialization) I know to be [pg 016] genuine. I do not at all mean by this that I know that the 'spiritualistic' interpretation of them is the true one. I mean only that they are genuine phenomena; that they have occurred; that they are not tricks or the result of fraud."

In the *Forum* of December, 1889, p. 455, the same writer describes his experience at the house of a friend with whom he had been acquainted eight or ten years. When about to depart, he thought he would try an experiment. He says:—

> "She and I stood at opposite ends of the table at which we had been sitting. Both of us having placed the tips of our fingers lightly on the top of the table, I spoke, as if addressing some unseen force connected with the table, and said: 'Now I must go; will you not accompany me to the door?' The door was ten or fifteen feet distant, and was closed. The table started. It had no casters, and in order to make it move as it did, we should have had to go behind and push it. As a matter of fact we led it, while it accompanied us all the way, and struck against the door with considerable force."

From the same article, p. 456, we quote again:—

> "I add one more experiment of my own. I sat one day in a heavy, stuffed armchair. The psychic sat beside me, and laying his hand on the back of the chair, gradually raised it. Immediately I felt and saw myself, chair and all, lifted into the air at least one foot from the floor. There was no uneven motion implying any sense of effort on the part of the lifting force; and I was gently lowered again to the carpet. This was in broad light, in a hotel parlor, and in presence of a keen-eyed lawyer friend. I could plainly watch the whole thing. No man living could have lifted me in such a position, and besides, I saw that the psychic made not the slightest apparent effort. Nor was there any machinery or preparation of any kind. My companion, the lawyer, on going away, speaking in reference to the whole sitting, said: 'I've seen enough

evidence to hang every man in the State—enough to prove *anything exceptingthis*.'

[pg 017]

"Professor Crookes, of London, relates having seen and heard an accordion played on while it was enclosed in a wire net-work, and not touched by any visible hand. I have seen an approach to the same thing. In daylight I have seen a man hold an accordion in the air, not more than three feet away from me. He held it by one hand, grasping the side opposite to that on which the keys were fixed. In this position, it, or something, played long tunes, the side containing the keys being pushed in and drawn out without any contact that I could see. I then said, 'Will it not play for me?' The reply was, 'I don't know: you can try it.' I then took the accordion in my hands. There was no music; but what did occur was quite as inexplicable to me, and quite as convincing as a display of some kind of power. I know not how to express it, except by saying that the accordion was seized as if by some one trying to take it away from me. To test this power, I grasped the instrument with both hands. The struggle was as real as though my antagonist was another man. I succeeded in keeping it, but only by the most strenuous efforts.

"On another occasion I was sitting with a 'medium.' I was too far away for him to reach me, even had he tried, which he did not do; for he sat perfectly quiet. My knees were not under the table, but were where I could see them plainly. Suddenly my right knee was grasped as by a hand. It was a firm grip. I could feel the print and pressure of all the fingers. I said not a word of the strange sensation, but quietly put my right hand down and clasped my knee in order to see if I could feel anything on my hand. At once I felt what seemed like the most delicate finger tips playing over my own fingers and gradually rising in their touches toward my wrist. When this was reached, I felt a series of clear, distinct, and definite pats, as though made by a hand of fleshy vigor. I made no motion to indicate what was going on, and said not a word until the sensation had passed. All this while I was carefully watching my hand, for it was plain daylight, and it was in full view; but I saw nothing."

We need not multiply evidence on this point. A remark by T. J. Hudson ("Law of Psychic Phenomena," [pg 018] p. 206, McClurg & Co., Chicago, 1894) may fitly close this division of the subject. He says:—

"I will not waste time, however, by attempting to prove by experiments of my own, or of others, that such phenomena do occur. It is too late for that.

The facts are too well known to the civilized world to require proof at this time. The man who denies the phenomena of spiritism to-day is not entitled to be called a skeptic, he is simply ignorant; and it would be a hopeless task to attempt to enlighten him."

A Manifestation of Intelligence.

From the testimony already given it is evident that there is connected with Spiritualism an agency that is able to manifest power and strength beyond anything that human beings, unaided, are able to exert. It is just as evident that the same agency possesses intelligence beyond the power of human minds. Indeed, this was the very feature that first brought it to the attention of the public. Spiritualism, as the reader is doubtless aware, originated in the family of Mr. John D. Fox, in Hydesville, near Rochester, N. Y., in the spring of 1848. Robert Dale Owen, in his work called "Footfalls on the Boundary of Another World," p. 290, has given a full narration of the circumstances attending this remarkable event. The particulars, he states, he had from Mrs. Fox, and her two daughters, Margaret and Kate, and son, David. The attention of the family had been attracted by strange noises which finally assumed the form of raps, or muffled footfalls, and became very annoying. Chairs were [pg 019] sometimes moved from their places, and this was once also the case with the dining-room table. Heard occasionally during February, the disturbance so increased during the latter part of March, as seriously to break the nightly repose of the family. But as these annoyances occurred only in the night-time, all the family hoped that soon, by some means, the mystery would be cleared away. They did not abandon this hope till Friday, the 31st of March, 1848. Wearied by a succession of sleepless nights, the family retired early, hoping for a respite from the disturbances that had harassed them. In this they were doomed to especial disappointment. We can do no better than to let Mr. Owen continue the narrative, in his own words:—

> "The parents had removed the children's beds into their bedroom, and strictly enjoined them not to talk of noises, even if they heard them. But scarcely had the mother seen them safely in bed, and was retiring to rest herself, when the children cried out, 'Here they are again!' The mother chided them, and lay down. Thereupon the noises became louder and more startling. The children sat up in bed. Mrs. Fox called her husband. The night being windy, it was suggested to him that it might be the rattling of the sashes. He tried several to see if they were loose. Kate, the younger girl, happened to remark that as often as her father shook a window-sash, the noises seemed to reply. Being a lively child, and in a measure accustomed to what was going on, she turned

to where the noise was, snapped her fingers, and called out, 'Here, old Splitfoot, do as I do!' The knocking instantly responded.

"That was the very commencement. Who can tell where the end will be?

"I do not mean that it was Kate Fox, who thus, in childish jest, first discovered that these mysterious sounds [pg 020] seemed instinct with intelligence. Mr. Mompesson, two hundred years ago, had already observed a similar phenomenon. Glanvil had verified it. So had Wesley, and his children. So we have seen, and others. But in all these cases the matter rested there and the observation was not prosecuted further. As, previous to the invention of the steam engine, sundry observers had trodden the very threshold of the discovery and there stopped, so in this case, where the royal chaplain, disciple though he was of the inductive philosophy, and where the founder of Methodism, admitting, as he did, the probabilities of ultramundane interference, were both at fault, a Yankee girl, but nine years old, following up more in sport than in earnest, a chance observation, became the instigator of a movement which, whatever its true character, has had its influence throughout the civilized world. The spark had been ignited,—once at least two centuries ago; but it had died each time without effect. It kindled no flame till the middle of the nineteenth century.

"And yet how trifling the step from the observation at Tedworth to the discovery at Hydesville! Mr. Mompesson, in bed with his little daughter (about Kate's age), whom the sound seemed chiefly to follow, 'observed that it would exactly answer, in drumming, anything that was beaten or called for.' But his curiosity led him no further.

"Not so Kate Fox. She tried, by silently bringing together her thumb and forefinger; whether she could obtain a response. Yes! It could *see*, then, as well as *hear*. She called her mother. 'Only look, mother,' she said, bringing together again her finger and thumb, as before. And as often as she repeated the noiseless motion, just as often responded the raps.

"This at once arrested her mother's attention. 'Count ten,' she said, addressing the noise. Ten strokes, distinctly given! 'How old is my daughter Margaret?' Twelve strokes. 'And Kate?' Nine. 'What can all this mean?' was Mrs. Fox's thought. Who was answering her? Was it only some mysterious echo of her own thought? But the next question which she put seemed to refute the idea. 'How many children have I?' she asked aloud. Seven strokes. 'Ah!' she thought, 'it can blunder sometimes.' [pg 021]

And then aloud, 'Try again.' Still the number of raps was seven. Of a sudden a thought crossed Mrs. Fox's mind. 'Are they all alive?' she asked. Silence for answer. 'How many are living?' Six strokes. 'How many are dead?' A single stroke. *She had lost a child.*

"Then she asked, 'Are you a man?' No answer. 'Are you a spirit?' It rapped. 'May my neighbors hear, if I call them?' It rapped again.

"Thereupon she asked her husband to call her neighbor, a Mrs. Redfield, who came in laughing. But her cheer was soon changed. The answers to her inquiries were as prompt and pertinent, as they had been to those of Mrs. Fox. She was struck with awe; and when, in reply to a question about the number of her children, by rapping four, instead of three, as she expected, it reminded her of a little daughter, Mary, whom she had recently lost, the mother burst into tears."

We have introduced this narrative thus at length not only because it is interesting in itself, but because it is of special interest that all the particulars of the origin, or beginning, of such a movement as this, should be well understood. The following paragraph will explain how it came to be called "The Rochester Knockings," under which name it first became widely known. It is from the "Report of the 37th Anniversary of Modern Spiritualism," held in Brooklyn, N. Y., March 31, 1885, and reported in the *Banner of Light*, the 25th of the following month:—

"After a song by J. T. Lillie, Mrs. Leah Fox Underhill, the elder of the three Fox sisters (who was on our platform), was requested to speak. Mrs. Underhill said that she was not a public speaker, but would answer any questions from the audience, and in response to these questions told in a graphic manner how the spirits came to their humble home in Hydesville, in 1848; how on the 31st of March the first intelligent communication from the spirit world came [pg 022] through the raps; how the family had been annoyed by the manifestations, and by the notoriety that followed; how the younger sisters, Catherine and Margaret, were taken to Rochester, where she lived, by their mother, hoping that this great and apparent calamity might pass from them; how their father and mother prayed that this cup might be taken away, but the phenomena became more marked and violent; how in the morning they would find four coffins drawn with an artistic hand on the door of the dining-room of her home in Rochester, of different sizes, approximating to the ages and sizes of the family, and these were lined with a pink color, and they were told that unless they made this great fact known, they would all speedily die, and enter the spirit-world.

"Gladly would they all have accepted this penalty for their disobedience in not making this truth known to the world. She told how they were compelled to hire Corinthian Hall in Rochester; how several public meetings were held in Rochester, culminating in the selection of a committee of prominent infidels, who, after submitting the Fox children to the most severe tests,—they being disrobed in the presence of a committee of ladies,—reported in their favor.... All the time she was on our platform, there was a continuous rapping by the spirits in response to what was being said by the several speakers, also in response to the singing, and all our exercises."

In the same volume of the *Forum* from which quotations have already been made, M. J. Savage states many facts which have a determinate bearing on the point now under consideration; namely, the intelligence manifested in the spiritual phenomena. From these we quote a few. He says (p. 452 and onward):—

"I am in possession of quite a large body of apparent facts that I do not know what to do with.... That certain things to me inexplicable have occurred, I believe. The negative opinion of some one with whom no such things have [pg 023] occurred, will not satisfy me.... I am ready to submit some specimens of those things that constitute my problem. They can be only specimens; for a detailed account of even half of those I have laid by, would stretch to the limits of a book.

"A merchant ship bound for New York was on her homeward voyage. She was in the Indian Ocean. The captain was engaged to be married to a lady living in New England. One day early in the afternoon he came, pale and excited, to one of his mates, and exclaimed, 'Tom, Kate has just died! I have seen her die!' The mate looked at him in amazement, not knowing what to make of such talk. But the captain went on and described the whole scene—the room, her appearance, how she died, and all the circumstances. So real was it to him, and such was the effect on him, of his grief, that for two or three weeks, he was carefully watched lest he should do violence to himself. It was more than one hundred and fifty days before the ship reached her harbor. During all this time no news was received from home. But when at last the ship arrived at New York, it was found that Kate did die at the time and under the circumstances seen and described by the captain off the coast of India. This is only one case out of hundreds. What does it mean? Coincidence? Just happened so? This might be said of one; but a hundred of such coincidences become inexplicable."

The following is another instance mentioned by the same writer:—

> "I went to the house of a woman in New York. She was not a professional. We had never seen each other before. We took seats in the parlor for a talk, I not looking for any manifestation. Raps began. I do not say whether they were really where they seemed to be or not; I know right well that the judgment is subject to illusion through the senses. But I was told a 'spirit friend' was present; and soon the name, time, and place of death, etc., were given me. It was the name of a friend I had once known intimately. But twenty years had passed since the old intimacy; she had lived in another State; I am certain that she and the [pg 024] psychic had never known or even heard of each other. She had died within a few months."

Mr. Savage then gives examples where the power in question was exclusively mental:—

> "The first time I was ever in the presence of a particular psychic, she went into a trance. She had never seen, and, so far as I know, had never had any way of hearing of my father, who had died some years previously. When I was a boy, he always called me by a special name that was never used by any other member of the family. In later years he hardly ever used it. But the entranced psychic said: 'An old gentleman is here,' and she described certain very marked peculiarities. Then she added: 'He says he is your father, and he calls you ——,' using the old childhood name of mine."

Again, same page:—

> "One case more, only, will I mention under this head. A most intimate friend of my youth had recently died. She had lived in another State, and the psychic did not know that such a person had ever existed. We were sitting alone when this old friend announced her presence. It was in this way: A letter of two pages was automatically written, addressed to me. I thought to myself as I read it,—I did not speak,—'Were it possible, I should feel sure she had written this.' I then said, as though speaking to her, 'Will you not give me your name?' It was given, both maiden and married name. I then began a conversation lasting over an hour, which seemed as real as any I ever have with my friends. She told me of her children, of her sisters. We talked over the events of boyhood and girlhood. I asked her if she remembered a book we used to read together, and she gave me the author's name. I asked again if she remembered the particular poem we were both specially fond of, and she named it at once. In the letter that was written, and in much of the

conversation, there were apparent hints of identity, little touches and peculiarities that would mean much to an acquaintance, but nothing to a stranger. I could not but be much impressed. Now in this case, I know that [pg 025] the psychic never knew of this person's existence, and of course not of our acquaintance."

Mr. Savage then mentions cases which he calls still more inexplicable, because the information conveyed was not known either to the psychic (which seems to be the new name for medium) or to himself. He says:—

"But one more case dare I take the space for, though the budget is only opened. This one did not happen to me, but it is so hedged about and checked off, that its evidential value in a scientific way is absolutely perfect. The names of some of the parties concerned *would be recognized in two hemispheres*. A lady and gentleman visited a psychic. The gentleman was the lady's brother-in-law. The lady had an aunt who was ill in a city two or three hundred miles away. When the psychic had become entranced, the lady asked her if she had any impression as to the condition of her aunt. The reply was, 'No.' But before the sitting was over, the psychic exclaimed, 'Why, your aunt is here! She has already passed away.' 'This cannot be true,' said the lady; 'there must be a mistake. If she had died, they would have telegraphed us immediately.' 'But,' the psychic insisted, 'she is here. And she explains that she died about two o'clock this morning. She also says that a telegram has been sent, and you will find it at the house on your return.'

"Here seemed a clear case for a test. So while the lady started for her home, her brother-in-law called at the house of a friend and told the story. While there the husband came in. Having been away for some hours he had not heard of any telegram. But the friend seated himself at his desk and wrote out a careful account, which all three signed on the spot. When they reached home,—two or three miles away,—there was the telegram confirming the fact and the time of the aunt's death, precisely as the psychic had told them.

"Here are most wonderful facts. How shall they be accounted for? I have not trusted my memory for these things, but have made careful record at the time. I know [pg 026] many other records of a similar kind kept by others. They are kept private. Why? The late Rev. J. G. Wood, of England, the world-famous naturalist, once said to me: 'I am glad to talk of these things to any one who has a right to know. But I used to call everybody a fool who had anything to do with them; and with a smile—"I do not enjoy being called a fool."'

> "Psychic and other societies that advertise for strange phenomena, must learn that at least a respectful treatment is to be accorded, or people will not lay bare their secret souls. And then, in the very nature of the case, these experiments concern matters of the most personal nature. Many of the most striking cases people will not make public. In some of those above related, I have had so to veil facts, that they do not appear as remarkable as they really are. The whole cannot be told."

A quotation from this same writer ("Automatic Writing," page 14), says:—

> "I am in possession of a respectable body of facts that I do not know how to explain except on the theory that I am dealing with some invisible intelligence. I hold that as the only tenable theory I am acquainted with."

In the same work (page 19), the author, Mrs. S. A. Underwood, as the result of her communications from spirits, says:—

> "Detailed statements of facts unknown to either of us [that is, herself and her 'control'], but which weeks afterward were learned to be correct, have been written, and repeated again and again, when disbelieved and contradicted by us."

On this point, also, as on the preceding, testimony need not be multiplied. The facts are too well known and too generally admitted to warrant the devotion of further space to a presentation of the [pg 027] evidence. *The question must soon be met, What is the source of the power and intelligence thus manifested?* But this may properly be held in abeyance till we take a glance at:

The Progress of Spiritualism.

during the fifty years of its modern history. It began in a way to excite the wonder and curiosity of the people, the very elements that would give wings to its progress through the land. Men suddenly found their thoughts careering through new channels. An unseen world seemed to make known its presence and invite investigation. As the phenomena claimed to be due to the direct agency of spirits, the movement naturally assumed the name of "Spiritualism." It was then hailed by multitudes as a new and living teacher, come to clear up uncertainties and to dispel doubts from the minds of men. At least an irrepressible curiosity was everywhere excited to know what the new "ism" would teach concerning that invisible world which it professed to have come to open to the knowledge of mankind. Everywhere men sought by what means they could come into communication with the spirit realm. Into whatever place the news entered, circles were formed, and the number of converts outstripped the pen of the enroller. It gathered adherents from every walk of life—from the higher classes as well as the lower; the educated, cultured, and refined, as well as the uncultivated and ignorant; from ministers, lawyers, physicians, judges, [pg 028] teachers, government officials, and all the professions. But the individuals thus interested, being of too diverse and independent views to agree upon any permanent basis for organization, the data for numerical statistics are difficult to procure. Various estimates, however, of their numbers have been formed. As long ago as 1876, computations of the number of Spiritualists in the United States ranged from 3,000,000 by Hepworth Dixon, to 10,000,000 by the Roman Catholic council at Baltimore. Only five years from the time the first convert to Modern Spiritualism appeared, Judge Edmonds, himself an enthusiastic convert, said of their numbers:—

> "Besides the undistinguished multitudes, there are many now of high standing and talent ranked among them,—doctors, lawyers, and clergymen in great numbers, a Protestant bishop, the learned and reverend president of a college, judges of our higher courts, members of Congress, foreign ambassadors, and ex-members of the United States Senate."

Up to the present time, it is not probable that the number of Spiritualists has been much reduced by apostasies from the faith, if such it may be called; while the movement itself has been growing more prominent and becoming more widely known every year. The conclusion would therefore inevitably follow that its adherents must now be more numerous than ever before. A letter addressed by the writer to the publishers of the *Philosophical Journal*, Chicago, on this point, received the following reply, dated Dec. 24, 1895:—

[pg 029]

> "Being unorganized, largely, no reliable figures can be given. Many thousands are in the churches, and are counted there. It is *claimed* that there are about five million in the United States, and over fifty million in the world."

The *Christian at Work* of Aug. 17, 1876, under the head of "Witches and Fools," said:—

> "But we do not know how many judges, bankers, merchants, prominent men in nearly every occupation in life, there are, who make it a constant practice to visit clairvoyants, sightseers, and so-called Spiritual mediums; yet it can scarcely be doubted that their name is legion; that not only the unreligious man, but professing Christians, men and women, are in the habit of consulting spirits from the vasty deep for information concerning both the dead and the living. Many who pass for intelligent people, who would be shocked to have their Christianity called in question, are constantly engaged in this disreputable business."

The following appeared some years ago, in the San Francisco *Chronicle*:—

> "Until quite recently, science has coldly ignored the alleged phenomena of Spiritualism, and treated Andrew Jackson Davis, Home, and the Davenport brothers, as if they belonged to the common fraternity of showmen and mountebanks. But now there has come a most noteworthy change. We learn from such high authority as the *Fortnightly Review* that Alfred R. Wallace, F. R. S.; William Crookes, F. R. S. and editor of the *Quarterly Journal of Science*; W. H. Harrison, F. R. S. and president of the British Ethnological Society, with others occupying a high position in the scientific and literary world, have been seriously investigating the phenomena of spiritism. The report which those learned gentlemen make is simply astounding. There is no

fairy tale, no story of myth or miracle, that is more incredible than their narrative. They tell us in grave and sober speech, that the spirit of a girl who died a hundred years ago, appeared to them in visible form. She talked with them, gave them locks of her hair, pieces of her dress, and her autograph. They [pg 030] saw her in bodily presence, felt her person, heard her voice; she entered the room in which they were, and disappeared without the opening of a door. The savants declare that they have had numerous interviews with her under conditions forbidding the idea of trickery or imposture.

"Now that men eminent in the scientific world have taken up the investigation, Spiritualism has entered upon a new phase. It can no longer be treated with silent contempt. Mr. Wallace's articles in the *Fortnightly* have attracted general attention, and many of the leading English reviews and newspapers are discussing the matter. The New York *World* devotes three columns of its space to a summary of the last article in the *Fortnightly*, and declares editorially that the 'phenomena' thus attested 'deserve the rigid scientific examination which Mr. Wallace invites for them.' This is treating the matter in the right way. Let all the well-attested facts be collected, and then let us see what conclusions they justify. If spirit communication is a fact, it is certainly a most interesting one. In the language which the World attributes to John Bright, 'If it is a fact, it is the one besides which every other fact of human existence sinks into insignificance.' "

One of the reasons why it would be quite impossible to state the number of real Spiritualists in our land to-day has already been hinted at in a foregoing extract. It is that "many thousands," and we think the number might in all probability be raised to millions, who are in reality Spiritualists, do not go by that name. They are in the various churches, and are counted there. Yet they believe the phenomena of Spiritualism, accept its teachings in their own minds, and quietly and constantly, as the *Christian at Work* avers, consult clairvoyants and mediums, in quest of knowledge. The grosser features of the teachings of Spiritualism which were painfully prominent [pg 031] in its earlier stages, which there is no reason to believe are discountenanced or abandoned either in theory or practice, are relegated to an invisible background, while in its outward aspect it now poses in the attitude of piety and the garb of religion. It even professes to adopt some of the more prominent and popular doctrines of Christianity. In this phase the average churchgoer cannot see why he may not accept all that Spiritualism has to give, and still retain his denominational relationship. Besides this, the coming to light, every now and then, of the fact that some person of national or world-wide fame is a Spiritualist, adds popularity and gives a new impetus to the movement. Such instances may be named as the founder of the Leland Stanford University, of California; the widow of ex-Vice-President Hendricks, of Indiana, who, it is said, is carrying on some very successful financial transactions by direction from the spirit world; and Mr. W. T. Stead, London editor of the *ReviewofReviews*, who, in 1893 started a new quarterly, called *TheBor derLand*, to be devoted to the advocacy of the philosophy of Spiritualism, which he had then but recently espoused. In other countries it has invaded the ranks of the nobility, and even seated itself on the thrones of monarchs. The late royal houses of France, Spain, and Russia are said, by current rumor, to have sought the spirits for knowledge. No cause could covet more rapid and wide-spread success than this has enjoyed.

Chapter Two.

What is the Agency in Question?

Having now shown that there are connected with Spiritualism supermundane phenomena that cannot be denied, and equally evident superhuman intelligence, sufficient to give to the movement unprecedented recognition in all the world, the way is open for the most important question that can be raised concerning it, and one which now demands an answer; and that is, What is the agency by which these phenomena are produced, and by which this intelligence is manifested? This question must be examined with the utmost care, and, if possible, a decision be reached of the most assuring certainty; for, as Mr. M. J. Savage says, "Spiritualism is either a grand truth or a most lamentable delusion."

It is proper that the claim which Spiritualism puts forth for itself, in this regard, should first be heard. This is so well known that it scarcely need be stated. It is that there is in every human being a soul, or spirit, which constitutes the real person; that this soul, or spirit, is immortal; that it manifests itself through a tangible body during this earth life, and when that body dies, passes unscathed into the unseen world, into an enlarged sphere of life, activity, and [pg 033] intelligence; that in this sphere it can still take cognizance of earthly things, and communicate with those still in the flesh, respecting scenes which it has left, and those more interesting conditions still veiled from mortal sight; that it is by these disembodied, or "discarnated" spirits that raps are given, objects moved, intelligence manifested, secrets revealed, slates written, voices uttered, faces shown, and epistles addressed to mortals, as friend would write to friend. If this be true, it opens what would indeed be considered a grand avenue of consolation to bereaved hearts, by giving them evidence that their departed friends still lived; that they recognized, loved, and accompanied them, and delighted still to counsel and instruct them. If not true, it is a masterpiece of superhuman craft and cunning; for it takes Christendom on the side where it is least guarded; as the view is everywhere held that the dead are conscious, and the only question would be as to their power to communicate with persons still living in the body; and it throws its arms around the individual when the heart is the most tender, when plunged into a condition in which every pang of bereaved sorrow, every tie of affection, and every throb of love, press him to crave with all his being that communication with the dead may be proved a fact, and to constrain him to accept the doctrine, unless kept from it by some power stronger than the cords that bind heart to heart in deathless love. If it be a deception, it occupies a vantage ground before which men may well tremble.

[pg 034]
But, as has been already stated, the question is here to be discussed from the standpoint of the Bible; the Bible is to be taken as the standard of authority by which all conflicting claims respecting the nature of man, must be decided. The authenticity of the Scriptures, in reference to those who deny their authority, is an antecedent question, into the discussion of which it is not the province of this little work to enter. A word, however, by way of digression, may be allowed in reference to its authorship.

Credentials of the Bible.

1. The Bible claims to be the word of God. Those who wrote it assert that they wrote as they "were moved by the Holy Ghost;" and they append to what they utter, a "Thus saith the Lord."

2. If it is not what it claims to be, it is an *imposture* invented by *deceivers* and *liars*.

3. *Good* men would not deceive and lie; therefore they were not the ones who invented the Bible.

4. If, therefore, it was invented by men at all, it must have been invented by *bad* men.

5. All liars and religious impostors are bad men; but—

6. The Bible repeatedly and most explicitly forbids lying and imposture, under the threatening of most condign punishment.

7. Would, therefore, liars and impostors invent a book which more than any other book ever written, denounces lying and imposture, thus condemning [pg 035] themselves to the severest judgments of God, and at last to eternal death?

8. If, then, the Bible is not the invention of good men,—because such men would not lie and deceive; nor of evil men,—because such men would not condemn themselves; nor of good or evil angels, for the same reasons, who else can be its author, but he who claims to be, that is, the living God?

9. If, therefore, from the very nature of the case, it must be God's book, why not believe it, and obey it?

To return: Appeal is therefore made to the Bible; and the object is to learn what the Bible teaches about Spiritualism. When the claim is put forth that it is the disembodied spirits of dead men who make the communications, the Bible reader is at once aware of a conflict of claims. In times when the Bible was written, there were practices among men which went under the names of "enchantment," "sorcery," "witchcraft," "necromancy," "divination," "consulting with familiar spirits," etc. These practices were all more or less related, but some of them bear an unmistakable meaning. Thus, "necromancy" is defined to mean "a pretended communication with the dead." A "familiar spirit" was "a spirit or demon supposed to attend on an individual, or to come at his call; the invisible agent of a necromancer's will."—*Century Dictionary.* Spiritualists do not deny that their intercourse with the invisible world comes under some, at [pg 036] least, of these heads. But all such practices the Bible explicitly forbids.

Deut. 18:9-12: "There shall not be found among you any one that maketh his son or his daughter to pass through the fire, or that useth divination, or an observer of times, or an enchanter, or a witch, or a charmer, or a consulter with *familiar spirits*, or a wizard, or a *necromancer*. For all that do these things are an abomination unto the Lord." Lev. 19:31: "Regard not them that have familiar spirits, neither seek after wizards, to be defiled by them: I am the Lord your God." See also, 2 Kings 21:2, 6, 9, 11; Rev. 21:8; Gal. 5:19-21; Acts 16:16-18; etc. Thus plainly in both the Old and New Testaments, are these practices forbidden.

An Impossibility.

But why does the Bible forbid such practices as necromancy, or a "pretended" communication with the dead?—Because it would be only a pretense at best; for such communication is impossible. The dead are unconscious in their graves, and have no power to communicate with the living. Let this truth be once established, and it is the death-blow to the claims of Spiritualism, in the cases of all who will receive it. Allusion has already been made to a popular and wide-spread dogma in the Christian church which furnishes a basis for Spiritualism. It is that the soul is immortal, and that the dead are conscious. Spirits make known their presence, and claim to be the spirits of persons who have once lived [pg 037] here in human bodies. Now if the Bible teaches that there is no such thing as a disembodied human spirit, a knowledge of that fact would enable one to detect at once the imposture of any intelligence which from behind the curtain should claim to be such spirit. Any spirit seeking the attention of men in this life, and claiming to be what the Bible says does not exist, comes with a falsehood on its lips or in its raps, if the Bible is true, and thus reveals its real character to be that of a deceiver. In this case the Bible believer is armed against the imposture. No man likes to be fooled. No matter therefore how nice the communicating intelligence may seem, how many true things it may say, or how many good things it may promise, the conviction cannot be evaded that no real good can be intended or conferred by any spirit, or whatever it may be, masquerading under the garb of falsehood, or pretending to be what it is not. On such a foundation no stable superstructure can be reared. It becomes a death-trap, sure to collapse and involve in ruin all those who trust therein.

It is very desirable that the reader comprehend the full importance of the doctrine, as related to this subject, that the dead are unconscious and that they have no power to communicate with the living. This being established, it sweeps away at one stroke the entire foundation of Spiritualism. Evidence will now be presented to show that this is a Bible doctrine; and wherever this is received, the fabric of Spiritualism from base to finial falls; it cannot [pg 038] possibly stand. But where the doctrine prevails that only the thin veil that limits our mortal vision, separates us from a world full of the conscious, intelligent spirits of those who have departed this life, Spiritualism has the field, beyond the possibility of dislodgment. When one believes that he has disembodied spirit friends all about him, how can he question that they are able to communicate with him? and when some unseen intelligence makes its presence known, and claims to be one of those friends, and refers to facts or scenes, known only to them two, how can the living dispute the claim? How can he refuse to accept a claim, which, on his own hypothesis, there is no conceivable reason to deny? But if the spirits are not what they claim to be, how shall the inexplicable phenomena attending their manifestations be explained?—The Bible brings to view other agencies, not the so-called spirits of the departed, to whose working all that has ever been manifested which to mortal vision is mysterious and inexplicable, may be justly attributed.

The Soul Not Immortal.

Spiritualism declares it to be the great object of its mission, to prove the immortality of the soul, which, it says, is not taught in the Scriptures with sufficient clearness, and is not otherwise demonstrated. It well attributes to the Scriptures a lack of plain teaching in support of that dogma; and it would have stated more truth, if it had said that the [pg 039] Scriptures nowhere countenance such a doctrine at all. But, it is said, the Scriptures are full of the terms, "soul" and "spirit." Very true; but they nowhere use those terms to designate such a part of man as in common parlance, and in popular theology, they have come to mean. The fact is, the popular concept of the "soul" and "spirit" has been formulated entirely outside the Bible. Sedulously, unremittingly, for six thousand years, the idea has been inculcated in the minds of men, from the cradle to the grave, that man is a dual being, consisting of an outward body which dies, and an inward being called "soul," or "spirit," which does not die, but passes to higher spirit life, when the body goes into the grave. The father of this doctrine is rarely referred to by its believers, as authority, possibly through a little feeling of embarrassment as to its parentage; for he it was who announced it to our first parents in these words: "Ye shall not surely die!" Gen. 3:4. When men began to die, it was a shrewd stroke of policy on the part of him who had promised them that they should not die, to try to prove to those who remained that the others had not really died, but only changed conditions. It is no marvel that he should try to make men believe that they possessed an immaterial, immortal entity that could not die; but, in view of the ghastly experiences of the passing years, it is the marvel of marvels that he should have succeeded so well. The trouble now is that men take these meanings which have been devised and fostered into [pg 040] stupendous strength outside the pale of Bible teaching, and attach them to the Bible terms of "soul" and "spirit." In other words, the mongrel pago-papal theology which has grown up in Christendom, lets the Bible furnish the terms, and paganism the definitions. But from the Bible standpoint, these definitions do not belong there; they are foreign to the truth, and the Bible does not recognize them. They are as much out of place as was the inventor of them himself in the garden of Eden. Let the Bible furnish its own definitions to its own terms, and all will be clear. The opinion of John Milton, the celebrated author of Paradise Lost, is worthy of note. In his "Treatise on Christian Doctrine," Vol. I, pp. 250, 251, he says:—

> "Man is a living being, intrinsically and properly one individual, not compound and separable, not, according to the common opinion, made up and framed of two distinct and different natures, as of body and soul, but the whole man is soul, and the soul, man; that is to say, a body or substance, individual, animated, sensitive, and rational."

In this sense the word is employed many times; but whoever will trace the use of the words "soul" and "spirit" through the Bible, will find them applied also to a great variety of objects; as, person, mind, heart, body (in the expression "a dead body"), will, lust, appetite, breath, creature, pleasure, desire, anger, courage, blast, etc., etc., in all nearly fifty different ways. But it is a fact which should be especially noted, that in not a single instance is there the least hint given that anything expressed by these [pg 041] terms is capable of existing for a single moment, as a conscious entity, or in any other condition, *without the body*! This being so, none of these, according to the Bible, are the agency claimed to be present in Spiritualism.

Another fact in reference to this point, should be allowed its decisive bearing. The question now under investigation is, Is the soul immortal, as Spiritualism has taken upon itself to teach, and claims to demonstrate? The Bible is found to be so lavish in the use of the terms "soul" and "spirit," that these words occur in the aggregate, *seventeen hundred times*. Seventeen hundred times, by way of description, analysis, narrative, historical facts, or declarations of what they can do, or suffer, the Bible has something to say about "soul" and "spirit." The most important question to be settled concerning them, certainly, is whether they are immortal or not. Will not the Bible, so freely treating of these terms, answer this question? Very strange, indeed, if it does not. But does it once affirm that either the soul or the spirit is immortal?—*Not once!* Does it ever apply to them the terms "eternal," "deathless," "neverdying," or any word that bears the necessary meaning of immortal?—Not in a single instance. Does it apply to them any term from which even an inference, necessary or remote, can be drawn that they are immortal? Even reduced to this attenuated form, the answer is still an emphatic and overwhelming, *No!* Well, then, does it say *anything* about the nature and capabilities of existence [pg 042] of that which it denominates soul or spirit?—Yes; it says the soul is in danger of the grave, may die, be destroyed, killed, and that the spirit may be wounded, cut off, preserved, and so, conversely, made to perish.

It is sometimes claimed that it is not necessary that the Bible should affirm the immortality of the soul, because it is so self-evident a fact that it is taken for granted. But no one surely can suppose that the immortality of the soul is more self-evident than that of Jehovah; yet the Bible has seen fit to affirm his immortality in most direct terms. 1 Tim. 1:17: "Now unto the King eternal, *immortal*, invisible, the only wise God, be honor and glory forever and ever. Amen." 1 Tim. 6:16: "Who only hath *immortality*, dwelling in the light which no man can approach unto; whom no man hath seen, nor can see: to whom be honor and power everlasting. Amen." Let, then, similar Bible testimony be found concerning the soul; that is, that it is "immortal," or "hath immortality," and the taken-for-granted device will not be needed.

[pg 043]

Chapter Three.

The Dead Unconscious.

From the fact now established that the soul is not immortal, it would follow as an inevitable conclusion, that the dead are not conscious in the intermediate state, and consequently cannot act the part attributed to them in modern Spiritualism. But there are some positive statements to which the reader's attention should be called, and some instances supposed to prove the conscious state which should be noticed.

1. *The Dead Know not Anything.*—As a sample of the way the Bible speaks upon this question, let the reader turn to the words of Solomon, in Eccl. 9:5, 6, 10: "For the living know that they shall die: but the dead know not anything, neither have they any more a reward; for the memory of them is forgotten. Also their love, and their hatred, and their envy, is now perished; neither have they any more a portion for ever in anything that is done under the sun.... Whatsoever thy hand findeth to do, do it with thy might; for there is no work, nor device, nor knowledge, nor wisdom, in the grave, whither thou goest."

This language is addressed to the real, living, intelligent, responsible man; and how could it be [pg 044] plainer? On the hypothesis of the commonly believed distinction between the soul and the body, this must be addressed to the soul; for the body considered as the mere material instrument through which the soul acts, is not supposed of itself to know anything. The body, as a body, independent of the soul, does not know that it shall die; but it is that which knows, while one is alive, that it shall die—it is that same intelligent being that, when dead, knows not anything. But the spirits in Spiritualism do know many things in their condition; therefore they are not those who have once lived on this earth, and passed off through death; for such, once dead, this scripture affirms, know not anything—they are in a condition in which there is "no work, nor device, nor knowledge, nor wisdom." This is a plain, straightforward, literal statement; there is no mistaking its meaning; and if it is true, then it is not true that the unseen agents working through Spiritualism, are the spirits of the dead.

2. *The Spirit Returns to God.*—Another passage from the same writer and the same book, may recur to the mind of the reader, as expressing a different and contradictory thought. Eccl. 12:7. "Then shall the dust return to the earth as it was: and the spirit shall return unto God who gave it." A careful analysis of this passage reveals no support for Spiritualism; for it does not say that the spirit, on returning to God, is conscious, or is capable of coming back and communicating with mortals. It is not denied that different component parts enter into [pg 045] the constitution of man; and that these parts may be separated. Solomon himself may therefore tell us what he means by the term "spirit" which he here uses. He employs the same word in chapter. 3:21 of this same book, but says that beasts have it as well as men. And then in verse 19, he explains what he means, by saying that they (man and the lower animals) *all* have one *breath*. The record of man's creation in Gen. 2:7, shows that a vitalizing principle, called the "breath of life," was necessary to be imparted to the organized body, before man became a living being; and this breath of life, as common to man and to all breathing animals, is described in Gen. 7:21, 22, by the term רוח (*ruahh*), the same word that is used for "breath," in Eccl. 3:19, "spirit," in verse 21, and "the spirit," which God gave to man, and which returns to God, in chapter 12:7. Thus it is clear that reference is here made simply to the "breath of life" which God at first imparted to man, to make him a living being, and which he withdraws to himself, in the hour of man's death. Job states the same fact, and describes the process, in chapter 34:14, 15: "If he [God] set his heart upon man, if he gather *unto himself* his [man's] spirit [same word] and his breath; ... man shall turn again unto dust." No one can fail to see here that Job refers to the same event of which Solomon speaks.

And at this point the question may as well be raised, and answered, Whence comes this spirit which is claimed to be the real man, capable of an [pg 046] independent and superior existence without the body? Bodies come into existence by natural generation; but whence comes the spirit? Is it a part of the body? If so, it cannot be immortal; for "that which is born of the flesh is flesh." John 3:6. Is it supplied to human beings at birth? If so, is there a great storehouse, somewhere, of souls and spirits, ready-made, from which the supply is drawn as fast as wanted in this world? And if so, further, is it to be concluded that all spirits have had a pre-existence? and then what was their condition in that state? And again, how does it happen, on this supposition, that this spirit in each individual exhibits so largely the mental and moral traits of the earthly parents? These hypotheses not being very satisfactory, will it be claimed that God creates these spirits as fast as children are born to need them? and if so, who brings them down just in the nick of time? and by what process are they incarnated? But if God has, by special act, created a soul or spirit for every member of the human family since Adam, is it not a contradiction of Gen. 2:2, which declares that *all* God's work of creation, so far as it pertains to this world, was *completed* by the close of the first week of time? Again, how many of the inhabitants of this earth are the offspring of abandoned criminality; and can it be supposed that God holds himself in readiness to create souls which must come from his hands pure as the dew of heaven, to be thrust into such vile tenements, and doomed to a life of wretchedness and woe at the bidding of [pg 047] defiant lust? The irreverence of the question will be pardoned as an exposure of the absurdity of that theory which necessitates it.

3. *The Spirits of Just Men Made Perfect.*—This expression is found in Heb. 12:23, and seems, by some, to recognize the idea that spirits can exist without the body, and are to be treated as separate entities. Thus interpreted it might appear to give some support to Spiritualism. But it will by no means bear such an interpretation. The apostle is contrasting the privileges of Christians in the present dispensation, with the situation of believers before the coming of Christ. What he sets forth are blessings to be enjoyed in the present tense. Yes, says one, that is just what I believe: We are come to spirits; they are all about us, and tip and talk and write for us at our pleasure. But hold! nothing is affirmed of spirits separately. The whole idea must be taken in. It is the "spirits of *just men* made perfect;" and the participle "made perfect" agrees with "just men," or literally "the just made perfect" (δικαίων τετελειωμένων), not with "spirits." It is the *men* who are made perfect to whom we are said to have come. But there are only two localities and two periods, in which men are anywhere in the Scriptures said to be made perfect. One is in this life and on this earth, and refers to

religious experience ("Be ye therefore perfect, even as your Father which is in heaven is perfect"); the other is not relative, but actual and absolute, and refers to the future immortal state when all the people of God [pg 048] will enter upon eternal life together ("God having provided some better thing for us, that they [the ancient worthies] without us should not be *made perfect*." Heb. 11:40). Thus, taken in either of the only two ways possible, the text furnishes no proof of Spiritualism. It doubtless refers to the present state, the expression, "spirits of just men," being simply a periphrasis for "just men," the same as the expression, "the God of the spirits of all flesh" (Num. 16:22), means simply "the God of all flesh," and the words "your whole spirit, and soul, and body" (1 Thess. 5:23), means simply the whole person.

4. *Spirits in Prison.*—The apostle Peter uses an expression, which, though perhaps not often quoted in direct defense of Spiritualism, is relied upon extensively in behalf of the doctrine of the conscious state of the dead, which, as already shown, is the essential basis of Spiritualism. And such texts as these are here noticed to show to the general reader, that the Bible contains no testimony in behalf of that doctrine, but positively forbids it, as further quotations will soon be introduced to show. The passage now in question is 1 Peter 3:19, where, speaking of Christ, it says: "By which also he went and preached unto the spirits in prison." By the use of strong assumption, and some lofty flights of the imagination, and keeping in the background the real intent of the passage, a picture of rather a lively time in the spirit world, can be constructed out of this testimony. Thus the spirits are said to be [pg 049] the disembodied spirits of those who were destroyed by the flood. See context. They were in "prison," that is, in hell. When Christ was put to death upon the cross, he immediately went by his disembodied spirit, down into hell and preached to those conscious intelligent spirits who were there, and continued that work till the third day when he was himself raised from the dead. A thought will show that this picture is wrong, (1) in the time, (2) in the condition of the people, (3) in the acting agent, and (4) in the end to be attained. Thus, when Christ had been put to death, he was "quickened" (or made alive), says the record, "by the Spirit." This was certainly not a personal disembodied spirit, but that divine agency so often referred to in the Scriptures. "By which," that is, this Spirit of God, he went and preached. Then he did not go personally on this work. The "spirits" were the antediluvians; for they were those who were

disobedient in the days of Noah. Now when were they preached to? Verse 20 plainly tells us it was "*when* once the longsuffering of God waited *in the days of Noah.*" In accordance with these statements now let another picture be presented: Christ, by his Spirit which was in Noah (1 Peter 1:11), and thus through Noah, preached to the spirits, or persons, in Noah's time, who were disobedient, in order to save all from the coming flood who would believe. They were said to be "in prison," though still living, because they were shut up under condemnation, and had only one hundred and twenty years granted them in which to [pg 050] repent or perish. Thus Christ was commissioned to preach to men said to be in prison, because in darkness, error, and condemnation, though they were still living in the flesh. Isa. 61:1. Dr. Adam Clarke, the eminent Methodist commentator (*in loco*), places the going and preaching of Christ in the days of Noah, and by the ministry of Noah for one hundred and twenty years, and not during the time while he lay in the grave. Then he says:—

> "The word πνεύμασι (spirits) is supposed to render this view of the subject improbable, because this must mean *disembodied* spirits; but this certainly does not follow; for the *spirits of just men made perfect* (Heb. 12:23), certainly means righteous men, and men *still in the church militant*: and the Father of spirits (Heb. 12:9) means men still in the body; and the God of the spirits of all flesh (Num. 16:22 and 27:16), means *men, not* in a disembodied state."[1]

5. *Cannot Kill the Soul.*—"Fear not them which kill the body, but are not able to kill the soul: but rather fear him which is able to destroy both soul and body in hell." Matt. 10:28. We know what it is to kill the body; and by association of ideas, it seems quite natural to form a like conception of the soul as something that can be treated in the same way. Then if the soul cannot be killed like the body, the conclusion seems easy of adoption that it lives right on, with all sensations preserved, as it was with the body before its death. If it were not for the pagan definition of "soul," which here comes in to change the current of thought, such [pg 051] conclusions drawn from this text would not be so prevalent; and a little attention to the scope of Christ's teaching here will readily correct the misapprehension. This is brought out clearly in verse 39: "He that findeth his *life* shall lose it: and he that loseth his *life* for my sake shall find it." This is easily understood. No

one will question what it is to lose his life; and Christ says that he who will do this for his sake, shall find it. Any one who has been put to death for his faith in the gospel has "lost his life" (had the body killed) for Christ's sake. But Christ says, Do not fear them, even if they do this. Why?—Because ye shall find it—the life you lost. When shall we find it?—In the resurrection. John 6:40; Rev. 20:4-6. The expression, "shall find it," thus becomes the exact equivalent of the words, "are not able to kill the soul;" that is, are not able to destroy, or prevent us from gaining that life he has promised, if we suffer men, for his sake, to "kill the body," or deprive us of our present life. The correctness of this view is demonstrated by the word employed in these instances. That word is ψυχή (*psuche*). It is properly rendered "life" in verse 39, and improperly rendered "soul" in verse 28. This lesson, that men should be willing to lose their life for Christ's sake, was considered so important that it is again mentioned in Matthew, and reiterated with emphasis by Mark, Luke, and John; and they all use this same word ψυχή, which is rendered "life." In one instance only in all these parallel passages have the [pg 052] translators rendered it "soul;" and that is Matt. 10:28, where it is the source of all the misunderstanding on that text.

6. *Souls Under the Altar.*—As a part of the events of the fifth seal as described in Rev. 6:9-11, John says he saw the souls of the martyrs under the altar, and heard them crying for vengeance. If they could do that, it is asked, cannot disembodied souls now communicate with the living? Not to enter into a full exposition of this scripture, and the inconsistencies such a view would involve, it is sufficient to ask if these were like the communicating spirits of the present day. How many communications have ever been received by modern Spiritualists from souls confined under an altar? In glowing symbolism, John saw the dead martyrs, as if slain at the foot of the altar; and by the figure of personification a voice was given to them, just as Abel's blood cried to God for vengeance upon his guilty brother (Gen. 4:10), and just as the stone is said to cry out of the wall, and the beam out of the timber to answer it. Hab. 2:11.

7. *The Medium of Endor.*—Aside from the direct teaching of the Scriptures, it is still held by some that there are scenes narrated in the Bible which show that the dead must be conscious. The first of these is the case of Saul and the woman of Endor, whom he consulted in order to communicate with

the prophet Samuel, as narrated in 1 Samuel 28. Here, it must be confessed, is brought to view an actual case of spirit manifestation, a specimen of [pg 053] ancient necromancy; for the conditions, method of procedure, and results, were just such as pertain to the same work in our own day. But then, as now, there was no truth nor good in it, as a brief review of the narrative will show. (1) Samuel was dead. (2) Saul was sore pressed by the Philistines. Verse 5. (3) God had departed from him. Verse 4. (4) He had cut off those who had familiar spirits and wizards, out of the land, because God had forbidden their presence in the Jewish theocracy, as an abomination. Verse 3; Lev. 19:31. (5) Yet in his extremity he had recourse to a woman with a familiar spirit, found at Endor. Verse 7. (6) She asked whom she should bring up, and Saul answered, Samuel. Verse 11. (7) Saul was disguised, but the familiar spirit told the woman it was Saul, and she cried out in alarm. Verse 12. (8) Saul reassured her, and the woman went on with the séance. Verse 10. (9) She announced a presence coming (not from heaven, nor the spheres, but) up out of the earth, and at Saul's request gave a description of him, showing that Saul did not himself see the form. Verse 13. (10) Saul "perceived" that it was Samuel (not by actual sight, but from the woman's description; for the Hebrew ידע and the Septuagint, γινωσκώ, signify to know, or perceive, by an operation of the mind.) Verse 14. (11) The woman supposed it was Samuel; Saul supposed it was Samuel; and that personation is, then, by the law of appearance, spoken of, in whatever it said or did, as Samuel; as, "Samuel said to [pg 054] Saul," etc. Verse 15. (12) Was Samuel really there as an immortal soul, a disembodied spirit, or as one raised from the dead?—No; because (*a*) immortal souls do not come up out of the ground, wrapped in mantles, and complain of being disquieted and brought up; (*b*) Samuel was a holy prophet, and if he was conscious in the spirit world, he would not present himself at the summons of a woman who was practicing arts which God had forbidden; (*c*) God having departed from Saul, and having refused to communicate with him on account of his sins, would not now suffer his servant Samuel to grant him the desired communication through a channel which he had pronounced an abomination; (*d*) Samuel was not present by a resurrection, for the Devil could not raise him, and God certainly would not, for such a purpose; besides Samuel was buried at Ramah, and could not be raised at Endor; (*e*) It was only the woman's familiar spirit, personating Samuel as he used to appear when alive—an aged man clothed with a mantle. His object was to make both the woman and Saul believe it was Samuel, when it was not, just as communicating spirits to-day try to palm themselves off for what they are not. As a specimen of ancient Spiritualism, this case is no particular honor to their cause; and as a proof of the immortality of the soul, and the conscious state of the dead, it is a minus quantity.

8. *The Transfiguration.*—Jesus took three of his disciples, Peter, James, and John, apart into a [pg 055] high mountain, and was transfigured before them; his face became as the sun, and his raiment was white as the light, just as it will be in the future kingdom of glory, which this scene was designed to represent. And there then appeared Moses and Elias talking with Christ. But Moses had died in the land of Moab nearly fifteen hundred years before, and it is at once concluded that the only way to account for his appearance on this occasion, is to suppose that he was still alive in the spirit world, and could appear in a disembodied state, and talk with Jesus as here represented. But such a conclusion is by no means necessary. Jesus was there in person, Elias was there in person; for he had not died, but had been translated bodily from this earth. Now it would be altogether incongruous to suppose that the third member of this glorious trio, apparently just as real as the others, was only a disembodied spirit; an immaterial phantom. Unless the whole scene was merely a vision brought before the minds of the disciples, Moses was as really there, in his own proper person, as Jesus and Elias. But there is no way in which he could thus be present, except by means of a resurrection from the dead; and that he had been raised, and was there as a representative of the resurrection, is proved, first by his actual presence on this occasion, and secondly, by the fact that Michael (Christ, who is "the resurrection and the life," John 11:25) disputed with the Devil (who has the power of death, Heb. 2:14) about the body of Moses. Jude 9. There could be [pg 056] no other possible ground of controversy about the body of Moses except whether or not Christ should give it life before the general resurrection. But Christ rebuked the Devil. Christ was not thwarted in this contest, but gave his servant life; and thus Moses could appear personally upon the mount. This makes the scene complete as a representation of the kingdom of God, as Peter says it was (2 Peter 1:16-18); namely, Christ the glorified King, Elias representing those who will be translated without seeing death, and Moses representing those who will be raised from the dead. These two classes embrace all the happy subjects of

that kingdom. This view of the matter is not peculiar to this book. Dr. Adam Clarke, on Matt. 17:3, says: "The body of Moses was probably raised again, as a pledge of the resurrection."[2] And Olshausen says: "For if we assume the reality of the *resurrection of the body*, and its glorification,—truths which assuredly belong to the system of Christian doctrine,—the whole occurrence presents no essential difficulties. The appearance of Moses and Elias, which is usually held to be the most unintelligible point in it, is as easily conceived of as possible, if we admit their bodily glorification."

Those passages which speak of Christ as the "first-fruits," the "first-born from the dead," the "first-born among many brethren," "of every creature," etc., refer only to the chief and pivotal importance [pg 057] of his own resurrection, as related to all others; and Acts 26:23 does not declare that Christ should be the first one to be raised from the dead, but that he first, by a resurrection from the dead, should show light to the Gentiles. (See the Greek of this passage.) These scriptures therefore prove no objection to the idea that Moses had been raised from the dead, and as a victor over the grave, appeared with Christ upon the mount. Thus another supposed stronghold affords no refuge for the conscious-state theory, or for Spiritualism.

9. *The Rich Man and Lazarus.*—With the features of this parable, as found in Luke 16, which is supposed to prove the dead conscious, and Spiritualism possible, the reader is doubtless familiar. It should ever be borne in mind that this is a parable; and in a parable, neither the parties nor the scenes are to be taken literally, and hence no doctrines can be built upon such symbolic representations. But not only is it a parable, but it is a parable based upon traditions largely entertained by the Jews themselves in the time of Christ. Thus T. J. Hudson ("Law of Psychic Phenomena," p. 385) says:—

> "It is a historical fact, nevertheless, that before the advent of Jesus, the Jews had become imbued with the Greek doctrine of Hades, which was an intermediate waiting station between this life and the judgment. In this were situated both Paradise and Gehenna, the one on the right, and the other on the left, and into these two compartments the spirits of the dead were separated, according to their deserts. Jesus found this doctrine already in existence, and in enforcing [pg 058] his moral precepts in his parables, he employed the

> symbols which the people understood, neither denying nor affirming their literal verity."

Thus Christ appealed to the people on their own ground. He took the views and traditions which he found already among them, and arranged them into a parable in such a way as to rebuke their covetousness, correct their notions that prosperity and riches in this life are tokens of the favor and approbation of God, and condemn their departure from the teachings of Moses and the prophets. As a parable, it is not designed to show the state of the dead, and the conditions that prevail in the spirit world. But if any persist that it is not a parable, but a presentation of actual fact, then the scene is laid, not in the intermediate state, but beyond the resurrection; for it is after the angels had carried Lazarus into Abraham's bosom. But the angels do not bear any one anywhere away from this earth, till the second coming of Christ and the resurrection of the dead. Matt. 24:30, 31; 1 Thess. 4:15-17. Finding no support in this portion of scripture for the conscious-state theory, with its spiritualistic possibilities, appeal is next made by the friends of that theory to the case of—

10. *The Thief on the Cross.*—Luke 23:39-43. When one of the malefactors who were crucified with Jesus, requested to be remembered when he should come into his kingdom, according to the record in the common version, the Lord replied, "To-day shalt thou be with me in paradise." To [pg 059] go from death into paradise the same day, means to go into the spirit world without a body, or discarnated, as Spiritualists claim. And so it would be if such was Christ's promise to the thief; but it was not.

The little adverb "to-day" holds the balance of power as to the meaning of this text. If it qualifies Christ's words, "Verily I say unto thee," it gives one idea; if it qualifies the words, "Thou shalt be with me in paradise," we have another and very different idea. And how shall the question of its relationship be decided?—It can be done only by the punctuation.

Here another difficulty confronts us; for the Greek was originally written in a solid line of letters, without any punctuation, or even division into words. Such being the case, the punctuation, and the relation of the qualifying word "to-day," must be determined by the context. Now it is a fact that

Christ did not go to paradise that day. He died, and was placed in the tomb, and the third day rose from the dead. Mary was the first to meet him, and sought to worship him. But he said, "Touch me not, for I am not yet ascended to my Father." John 20:17. Paradise is where the Father is (see 2 Cor. 12:2-4; Rev. 2:7; 22:1, 2), and if Christ had not been to his Father when Mary met him the third day after his crucifixion, he had not then been to paradise; therefore it is not possible that he made a promise to the thief on the day of his crucifixion, that he should be with him *that* day in paradise.

[pg 060]
But further, the day of the crucifixion was the day before the Sabbath; and it was not lawful to leave criminals on the cross during that day. John 19:31. If they were still living when the time came to take them from the cross, they were taken down, and their legs were broken to prevent their escape. The soldiers on this occasion broke the legs of the two thieves, because they were still alive; "but when they came to Jesus and saw that he was dead already, they brake not his legs." Verses 32, 33. The thief therefore lived over into the next day.

Thus there are two absolutely insuperable objections against allowing the adverb, "to-day," to qualify Christ's promise, "Thou shalt be with me in paradise:" (1) Christ did not go to paradise that day; and (2) The thief did not die that day. Before these facts the conscious-state argument built upon this incident, vanishes into thin air. Just place the comma (a punctuation mark not invented till 1490) after "to-day" instead of before it, and let that word qualify the verb "say" and emphasize the time when it was spoken, and all is harmonious. The thief's request did not pertain to that day, but looked forward to the time when Christ should come into his kingdom; and Christ's promise did not pertain to that day, but to the time in the thief's request; so he did not falsify it by not going to his Father for three days afterward. The thief is quietly slumbering in the tomb; but Christ is soon coming into his kingdom. Then the thief will be [pg 061] remembered, be raised from the dead, and be with Christ in that paradise into which he will then introduce all his people. Thus all is as clear as a sunbeam, when the text is freed from the bungling tinkering of men.

The strongest texts and incidents which are appealed to in defense of the conscious-state theory, have now been examined. If these do not sustain it, nothing can be found in the Bible which will sustain it. All are easily harmonized with these. Thus in Paul's desire to "depart and be with Christ" (Phil. 1:23), he does not there tell us *when* he will be with Christ; but he does tell us in many other places; and it is at the resurrection and the coming of Christ. Phil. 3:11; 1 Thess. 4:16, 17. When he speaks of our being clothed upon with our house from heaven (2 Cor. 5:2), he tells us that it is when "mortality" is "swallowed up of life." But that is only at the last trump. 1 Cor. 15:51-54. If we are told about the woman who had had seven husbands (Matt. 22:23-28), no hint is given of any reunion till after the resurrection. If God calls himself "not the God of the dead, but of the living" (Matt. 22:32), it is because he speaks of "those things that be not as though they were" (Rom. 4:17), and the worthies of whom this is spoken, are sure to live again (Heb. 11:15, 16), and hence are now spoken of as alive in his sight, because they are so in his purpose. Texts which speak of the departure and return of the soul (Gen. 35:18; 1 Kings 17:21, 22), are referable to the [pg 062] "breath of life," which is the meaning of the word in these instances rendered "soul."

Three passages only have been referred to, which declare positively that the dead know not anything. It was thought preferable to answer certain objections, before introducing further direct testimony. But there are many such passages, a few more of which will now be presented, as a fitting conclusion to this branch of the subject. The reader's careful attention is invited to a few of the various texts, and the conclusions that follow therefrom.

1. *Death and Sleep.*—Death, in numerous passages is compared to sleep, in contrast with the wakeful condition. See Ps. 13:3; Job 7:21; John 11:11; Acts 7:60; 1 Cor. 11:30; 15:51; 1 Thess. 4:14; etc. But there is only one feature in sleep by virtue of which it can be taken as a figure of death; and that is, the condition of unconsciousness which shuts up the avenues of one's senses to all one's environment. If one is not thus unconscious in death, the figure is false, and the comparison illogical and misleading.

2. *Thoughts Perish.*—So David testifies: "Put not your trust in princes, nor in the son of man, in whom there is no help. His breath goeth forth, he returneth to his earth; in that very day his thoughts perish." Ps. 146:3, 4. The word "thoughts" does not here mean simply the projects and purposes one has in view, which do often fail, when the author of them dies, but it is from a root which means the act of thinking, the operation of the mind; [pg 063] and in death, that entirely ceases. It cannot therefore be the dead who come out of the unseen with such intelligence as is shown in Spiritualism.

3. *Job's Statement.*—Speaking of a dead man, Job (14:21) says: "His sons come to honor, and he knoweth it not; and they are brought low, but he perceiveth it not of them." If the dead cannot take cognizance of matters of so much interest as these, how can they communicate with the living as the spirits do?

4. *No Remembrance of God.*—David, in Ps. 6:5 and 115:17, again testifies: "For in death there is no remembrance of thee: in the grave who shall give thee thanks?" "The dead praise not the Lord, neither any that go down into silence." Is it possible that any righteous man, if he is living and conscious after going into the grave, would not praise and give thanks to the Lord?

5. *Hezekiah's Testimony.*—Hezekiah was sick unto death. Isa. 38:1. But he prayed, and the Lord added to his days fifteen years. Verse 5. For this he praised the Lord, and gave his reasons for so doing in the following words (verses 18, 19): "For the grave cannot praise thee, death cannot celebrate thee: they that go down into the pit cannot hope for thy truth. The living, the living, he shall praise thee, as I do this day." This is a clear affirmation that in death he would not be able to do what he was able to do while living.

6. *New Testament Evidence.*—The New Testament bears a corresponding testimony on this subject. [pg 064] None will be saved except such as Christ raises up at the last day. John 6:39, 40. No one is to receive any reward before the resurrection. Luke 14:14; 2 Tim. 4:8. No one can enter God's kingdom before being judged; but there is no execution of judgment before the coming of Christ. 2 Tim. 4:1; Acts 17:31; Luke 19:35; etc. If there is no avenue to a future life by a resurrection, then all who have gone down in death are perished. 1 Cor. 15:18. Such texts utterly forbid the idea

of consciousness and activity, on the part of any of the human family, in death.

This part of the subject need not be carried further. It has been dwelt upon so fully simply because of its determinate bearing on the question under discussion. Spiritualism rests its whole title to credence on the claim that the intelligences which manifest themselves are the spirits of the dead. The Bible says that they are *not* the spirits of the dead. Then if the Bible is true, the whole system rests upon deception and falsehood. No one who believes this will tamper with Spiritualism. One cannot have Spiritualism and the Bible, too. One or the other must be given up. But he who still holds on to the theory that the dead are conscious, contrary to the testimony of the Scriptures has no shield against the Spiritualistic delusion, and the danger is that he will sooner or later throw the Bible away.

[pg 065]

Chapter Four.

They Are Evil Angels.

As the Bible plainly shows what the spirits which communicate are *not*, it just as clearly reveals also what they *are*; so that in no particular is one left to conjecture or guesswork. There is an order of beings brought to view in the Scriptures, above man but lower than God or Christ, called "angels." No Bible believer questions the existence of such beings. It is sometimes asserted that angels are departed human spirits; but this cannot be; for they appear upon the stage of action before a single human being had died, or a disembodied spirit could have existed. When the world was created, Job declares that "the morning stars sang together, and all the sons of God shouted for joy." These are two of the names applied to these beings, but they are also known by a number of others. They are 167 times called angels; 61 times, angel of the Lord; 8 times, angel of God; 17 times, his angels; 41 times, cherub and cherubim. There are also such names as seraphim, chariots, God's hosts, watchers, holy ones, thrones, dominions, principalities and powers,—all referring to the different orders of these heavenly beings.

A part of this host fell into sin, and thereby became evil, or fallen, angels. A reasonable statement [pg 066] of how this came about can be given, but no reason for the act itself. Sin cannot be explained. To explain it would be to give a reason for it; and to give a reason for it would be to excuse it; and then it would cease to be sin. In the beginning a condition existed which was in itself right and essential; but which nevertheless made sin possible. It is one of the inevitable conditions of the highest glory of God, that all his creatures should serve him from choice, under the law of love, and not by compulsion, as a machine, under the law of necessity. To secure this end, they must be made free moral agents. Thus to angels was given the freedom of the will, the same as to man. They were in a state of purity and happiness, with every condition favorable for a continuance in that condition; but in the free choices of their free wills, they of course had the power, if they should unaccountably see fit so to use it, to turn away from truth and right, and rebel against God. This some of them did. So we find Jude speaking of "the angels that kept not their first estate" (Jude 6), and Peter, of "the angels that sinned" (2 Peter 2:4); and these they further declare, were cast down to Tartarus, and are reserved in everlasting chains under darkness, unto the judgment of the great day.

There must have been to this rebellion an instigator and leader; and we accordingly find the Bible speaking of such a personage; the whole company being described as "the Devil and his angels." Our Lord pointed out this leader in evil, and his [pg 067] work, in John 8:44: "Ye are of your Father the Devil, and the lusts of your father ye will do. He was a murderer from the beginning, and abode not in the truth, because there is no truth in him. When he speaketh a lie, he speaketh of his own: for he is a liar and the father of it." This reveals the great facts in his case. He abode not in the truth. Then he was once in the truth; and as he is a liar, and the father of it, he was the first one to depart from truth and introduce falsehood and evil into the universe of God.

In Isaiah (14:12-14) this being is addressed as Lucifer, or the day-star; and the prophet exclaims, "How art thou fallen from heaven, 0 Lucifer, son of the morning! how art thou cut down to the ground, which didst weaken the nations!" The following verses indicate that the nature of his transgression was self-exaltation and pride of heart: "For thou hast said in thine heart, I will ascend into heaven, I will exalt my throne above the stars of God: I will sit also upon the mount of the congregation, in the sides of the north: I will ascend above the heights of the clouds; I will be like the Most High." Paul, in 1 Tim. 3:6, intimates that it was this pride that caused the ruin of this once holy being. Of an elder he says that he must not be a novice, "lest being lifted up with pride he fall into the condemnation of the Devil," or that sin for which the Devil was condemned.

In Ezekiel 28, Satan is again spoken of under the pseudonym of "the prince of Tyrus." Verse 2 [pg 068] shows his pride: "Because thine heart is lifted up, and thou hast said, I am a God, I sit in the seat of God," etc. Verses 12-15 describe his beauty, wisdom, and apparel, and his exalted office as a high cherub, before his sin and fall. Verse 15 reads: "Thou wast perfect in thy ways from the day thou wast created, till iniquity was found in thee."

These passages give us a sufficient idea of the origin of Satan and how such an incarnation of evil has come to exist. The Tartarus into which he and his angels were cast, according to Peter, is defined by leading lexicographers, as meaning the dark, void, interplanetary spaces, surrounding the world. Using the serpent as a medium, this apostate angel, thus cast out, plied our first parents with his temptation by preaching to them the immortality of the soul, "Thou shalt not surely die," and alas! seduced them also into rebellion. The dominion which was given to Adam (Gen. 1:28), Adam thus alienated to Satan, by becoming his servant; for Paul says, "Know ye not, that to whom ye yield yourselves servants to obey, his servants ye are to whom ye obey?" Rom. 6:16. Now, consequently, such titles as "prince of this world," "prince of the power of the air," "god of this world," etc., are applied to him, because he has by fraud usurped that place. John 14:30; Eph. 2:2; 2 Cor. 4:4. He, of course, employs "his angels" to co-operate with him in his nefarious work.

Thus clearly do we have set before us just the agencies,—the Devil and his angels,—which are [pg 069] adapted, both by nature and inclination, to carry on just such a work as is seen in Spiritualism. But how do we know, some one may ask, but that Spiritualism is the work of the good angels?— We know that it is not, because good angels do not lie. They never would come to men, professing to be the spirits of their dead friends, and imitate and personate them to deceive, knowing that the mediums did not know, and could not ascertain that they were altogether another and different order of beings. But the evil angels, led by the father of lies, and cradled, and drilled, and skilled, and polished, in the school of lying, would be delighted to deceive men in this very way, by pretending to be their dead friends, and then by working upon their affections and love for the ones they could skilfully personate, bring them under their influence and lead them captive at their will.

These evil angels are experts in deception. They have had six thousand years' experience. They are well acquainted with the human family. They can read character. They study temperament. They acquaint themselves minutely with personal history. They know a thousand things which only they and the individual they are trying to ensnare, are aware of. They know many things beyond the knowledge of men. They can easily carry the news of the decease of a friend, and the description of a death-bed scene, to other friends thousands of miles away, and months before the truth through ordinary channels can reach them, so that when it is verified, their influence over them may be increased. (See page 23.)

[pg 070]
There is nothing that has yet taken place, of however inexplicable a nature, and nothing which even the imagination may anticipate, which is not, and will not be, easily attributable to these unseen angels. They are lying spirits; for the fundamental principle on which they are acting is a lie; but they tell enough truth to sway and captivate the minds of men. It matters not how sacred the field in which they tread, nor how hallowed the associations which they invade, they press into every spot where it is possible, by spinning another thread, to strengthen their web of deception.

And in what dulcet and siren tones they woo their victims to lay aside all resistance to their influence, to become receptive and passive, and yield themselves to their control; and when they have them thus helpless in their arms, they deliberately and cruelly instil into their minds the virus of ungovernable lust, the leprosy of unconquerable rebellion against the government of Heaven. That this language does not misrepresent nor slander them, will be shown from their own testimony, before the close of this book.

The thought is not overlooked that many even of those who do not profess to be Spiritualists, deny the existence of any such being as a personal Devil, or of personal evil angels, his agents. He is no doubt well pleased with this, as such people can the more easily be made the victims of his wiles. But these same persons would no doubt acknowledge the existence, as real beings, of God, Christ, and the [pg 071] good angels. This fact being established, by parity of reasoning the Devil and his angels become real beings also. The same arguments which show that God and Christ exist as personal beings may be used to show that the Devil and his angels are personal beings also. He who denies that there is a personal Devil, must be prepared also to deny that there is a personal Christ. So far as the argument for personal existence is concerned, Christ and good angels stand on one side of the equation, and the Devil and his angels on the other; and whoever would rub out the one, must rub out the other also.

Christ said that he "beheld Satan as lightning fall from heaven." Luke 10:18. John in the Revelation (12:7) beheld a war in heaven. "Michael [Christ] and his angels fought against the dragon [Satan]; and the dragon fought, and his angels." On the ground that there is no Devil, this would be a wonderful battle—Christ and his angels, who are real beings, fighting furiously against myths and nonentities which have not even the substance of a phantom.

To endorse the doctrine of a personal Devil, is not to endorse the grossly absurd caricatures conjured up by morbid imaginations, and popular theology,—a being with bat's wings, horns, hoofs, and a dart-pointed tail. Yet upon such pictorial fables he doubtless looks with complacency; as they are calculated still further to destroy faith in his existence, and enable him the better to cover his tracks and carry on his work among men. Nevertheless [pg 072] the only rational hypothesis on which to account for the present condition of this world (which every one must admit is full of devilishness), the existence of evil, and the presence of sickness, suffering, and death, is the account the Bible gives us of fallen angels and fallen men. Unfallen angels are beings of mighty power. One of them slew in one night 185,000 Assyrians (2 Kings 19:35); and the one who appeared at the time of Christ's resurrection had a countenance like the lightning, and raiment white as snow, and before him the keepers of the tomb fell like dead men. Matt. 28:3, 4. A fall from their high estate, though it would impair their strength and power, cannot be supposed to have wholly deprived them of these qualities; therefore the fallen angels still have capabilities far superior to those of men. The only defense mankind has against them is found in

Christ, who circumscribes their power (for they are kept in chains, 2 Peter 2:4), and makes provision by which we may resist them. Eph. 6:11; James 4:6-8; 1 John 5:18. The question why they are permitted to continue finds solution in the thought that God is consistently giving to sin time and opportunity to develop itself, fully show its nature, and manifest its works, to all created intelligences, so that when it shall finally be wiped out of existence, with all its originators, aiders, and abetters, as in God's purpose it is to be (Rev. 20:14, 15; 2 Peter 3:7, 13; Rev. 5:13), there will ever after remain an object-lesson sufficient to safe-guard the universe against a repetition of the evil. [pg 073] Only some 6000 years are allotted to this work of evil; and 6000 years are as nothing compared with eternity.

Warnings Against Evil Spirits.

The Scriptures plainly point out the working of these agents of wickedness, and warn us against them. In 1 Tim. 4:1, we read: "Now the Spirit speaketh expressly, that in the latter times some shall depart from the faith, giving heed to seducing spirits, and doctrines of devils." This shows that these spirits make it an object to seduce, or deceive, to draw men away from the true faith, and cause them to receive, instead, the doctrines they teach, which are called "doctrines of devils;" and this scripture is written to put men on their guard against them.

Again Paul says: "For we wrestle not against flesh and blood, but against principalities, against powers, against the rulers of the darkness of this world, against spiritual wickedness [margin, 'wicked spirits'] in high places." Eph. 6:12. And he adjures his readers to put on the whole armor of God to be able to resist them.

The apostle Peter exhorts to the same purpose: "Be sober, be vigilant; because your adversary the devil, as a roaring lion, walketh about, seeking whom he may devour: whom resist steadfast in the faith." 1 Peter 5:8, 9. If our ears do not deceive us, a good deal of this roaring is heard in the ranks of Spiritualists, where, by invisible rapping, agitated furniture, clairvoyance, clairaudience, [pg 074] writing, speaking, marvels, and wonders, he seeks to set the world on tiptoe of curiosity and expectation, and bewilder men into a departure from the faith and the acceptance of the doctrines of devils. He is cunning enough not to "roar" in a way to frighten and repel, but only to attract attention, and lead multitudes, through an overweening curiosity and wonder at the marvels, to come thoughtlessly within the sphere of his influence.

The prophet Isaiah also has something to say directly upon this subject: "And when they shall say unto you, Seek unto them that have familiar spirits, and unto wizards that peep, and that mutter: should not a people seek unto their God? for the living to the dead?" Isa. 8:19. That is, is it consistent for living people to go to dead ones for their knowledge? The following verse shows where we should go for light and truth: "To the law and to the testimony: if they speak not according to this word, it is because there is no light in them." The time has certainly come when many are saying just what the text points out, and seeking to the dead, to familiar spirits, and wizards, for knowledge. Those practices which in the Bible are enumerated as "charming," "enchantment," "sorcery," "witchcraft," "necromancy," "divination," "consulting with familiar spirits," etc., are more or less related, and are all really from one source. So in modern times different names indicate substantially the same thing. Thus Mr. Hudson, in "Psychic Phenomena," p. v, says:—

> "It has, however, long been felt by the ablest thinkers of our time that all psychic manifestations of the human intellect, normal or abnormal, whether designated by the name of mesmerism, hypnotism, somnambulism, trance, spiritism, demonology, miracle, mental therapeutics, genius, or insanity, are in some way related."

Seven, at least, of the foregoing names are no doubt in the warp and woof of Spiritualism; and he might have added mind-reading and Christian Science. And Spiritualists admit that their work is the same as that described by the Bible terms above quoted. Thus, Allen Putnam, a Spiritualistic writer, says:—

> "The doctrine that the oracles, soothsaying, and witchcraft of past ages were kindred to these manifestations of our day, I, for one, most fully believe."

In a pamphlet by the same author, entitled, "Mesmerism, Spiritualism, Witchcraft, and Miracle," p. 6, he says:—

> "As seen by me now, Mesmerism, Spiritualism, Witchcraft, Miracles, all belong to one family, all have a common root, and are developed by the same laws."

To all these, therefore, the text under notice (Isa. 8:19, 20) applies. We are to bring them to the standard of "the law and the testimony," and "if they speak not according to this word ... there is no light in them." The living should not seek to the dead.

In Rev. 16:13, 14, the same spirits are again brought to view, and called "unclean spirits," and "spirits of devils." Their last work of deception is to go forth to the kings of the earth, and of the [pg 076] whole world, to gather them to the battle of the great day of God Almighty. Thus all that is revealed of them from beginning to end (and scriptures might be multiplied on the point) furnishes the most cogent reason why all should be keenly awake to their existence and their work, and be ever watchful against their influence and approach.

[pg 077]

Chapter Five.

What The Spirits Teach.

It has been shown in the preceding chapters that the unseen "controls" (the beings who control the mediums) in Spiritualism, are not the spirits of the dead, but are fallen angels or spirits of devils. This fact will be confirmed by a brief glance at some of their teachings; for we are to remember that if they speak not according to the law and the testimony there is no light in them. It matters not that what they teach may be supported by signs and wonders beyond the comprehension of the human mind. That is no guarantee of truth; for such phenomena are to be wrought, as will soon be shown, to prove a lie. The Lord anciently put his people on their guard in this respect. Deut. 13:1-3, 5: "If there arise among you a prophet, or a dreamer of dreams, and giveth thee a sign or a wonder, and the sign or the wonder come to pass, whereof he spake unto thee, saying, Let us go after other gods, which thou hast not known, and let us serve them; thou shalt not hearken unto the words of that prophet, or that dreamer of dreams: for the Lord your God proveth you, to know whether ye love the Lord your God with all your heart and with all your soul." "And that prophet, or that dreamer of [pg 078] dreams, shall be put to death; because he hath spoken to turn you away from the Lord your God, ... out of the way which the Lord thy God commanded thee to walk in."

Thus the fact that one who professed to be a prophet could perform a sign or wonder, showing his connection with some unseen power, was not enough to shield him from condemnation and punishment, if what he undertook to prove by that sign or wonder was contrary to the truth, and tended to lead away from God. The teaching of any system is an important part of the fruit it bears; and by that, according to our Lord's own rule, we are to judge it, and not by any power or mighty works connected with it, however wonderful they may be.

"'Tis not the broad phylactery
    Nor stubborn fasts, nor stated prayers
That make us saints. We judge the tree
    By what it bears."
—*Alice Carey.*

It is therefore pertinent to look sufficiently at the teachings of the spirits to ascertain their character. Here we shall find some most damaging testimony; for—

1. *They Deny God.*—It is no pleasure to transcribe the utterances of practical atheism; yet enough should be given to show what they teach on the great fundamental principles of Christianity. At a séance, reported in the *Banner of Light,* July 11, 1868, the following questions were addressed to the spirits, and the accompanying answers received:—

> "*Ques.*—It is said in the Bible that man is made in the image of God. Please tell us what that image is.

> "*Ans.*—He is made in the image of everything that ever was, that is, or that ever shall be. He holds within his caliber everything that exists, that ever has existed, or that ever will exist. Now, God is included in this. If he exists at all, he exists everywhere (and we have taken in everything), every place, every name, every condition. I believe that the human stands above all things else, and holds within its embrace all the past, present, and future. In this sense he is created and exists in the image of God.

> "*Q.*—What is God essentially?

> "*A.*—Everything. Essentially you are God, and I am God—the flowers, the grass, the pebbles, the stars, the moon, the sun, everything is God."

The Devil, through the serpent in the garden, taught Adam and Eve that the soul is immortal, and has transfused the same idea very successfully through paganism, Romanism, and Protestantism; but he also said, "Ye shall be as gods;" and now, it seems, he is trying to make the world swallow this other leg of his falsehood; but by putting it forth under the form of the old pagan pantheism, that everything is God, and God is everything, he betrays the lie he uttered in Eden; for in that case, Adam and Eve were no more gods after they ate than they were before.

Another séance, reported in the *Banner* about twenty years later than the one quoted above, April 28, 1888; an inquirer addressed to the "spirits" a question about God, and received answer, a portion of which is presented below:—

> "*Ques.*—Some Spiritualists, I learn, believe in a God; otherwise they would not pray to him—taking for granted that there is such a being. Please enlighten us.

> "*Ans.*—We have yet to come in contact with a thorough Spiritualist, one who understands something of spiritual life and the revelations made by returning spirits, who directly [pg 080] believes in a personal God. True, many Spiritualists and many returning spirits offer their invocations to the 'Great Supreme Spirit of all life and intelligence,' not because they expect to change the order of law, or to come into direct communication with, or nearness to, a Great Supreme Being, clothed in the image of man, but because they desire to enter an atmosphere of harmony, to uplift their own souls to a plane of thought which will bring spiritual inspiration to their minds. We make a distinction between that Great Supreme Overruling Force which we may call the Superior Spirit of Intelligence, Wisdom, and Love, and the personal Deity, clothed in the image of man, gigantic in stature, jealous and revengeful by nature, which has been set up and worshiped as the Christian Jehovah. We know of no Spiritualist—let us repeat it—who believes in such a personal God; but we can believe and accept the idea, though it may pass beyond almost our finite comprehension, that there is a grand universal Spirit permeating all forms of existence; that this great source of light, of activity and vitality vibrates with intelligence, and that it is superior to all organic forms, however grand they may prove to be."

The same views have been taught all along by the "spirits" of Spiritualism, as could be shown by extracts dating as far back as 1858, only ten years after the "Rochester Knockings." And though Spiritualism is now assuming more of the sedate speech of organized Christianity, the spirits do not modify their teaching in respect to God. In "Automatic, or Spirit, Writing," p. 148 (1896), are given many messages from the spirits through the mediumship of Mrs. S. A. Underwood, wife of the editor of the *Philosophical Journal*, Chicago. The "spirits" set forth their teaching in answer to questions by the medium, some of which have reference to God, though his name is not used. Thus on page 148, this conversation is given:
—

[pg 081]

"*Ques.*—You often in these communications speak of the binding laws of spiritual life—that because of them you cannot give us such and such information, etc. Now who makes those laws, and whence came they, and how are they taught?

"*Ans.*—Thou say'st 'who'—therefore we cannot answer. Go back to the first question and ask one at a time.

"*Q.*—Well, who makes the laws?

"*A.*—Spirits are not bondaged by *persons*.

"*Q.*—Then how do you come to know those laws?

"*A.*—Pharos will now answer. Spiritual laws are spiritually perceived, as soon as the physical perceptions are got rid of.

"*Q.*—Could you explain to us those laws?

"*A.*—Courses of teaching from our side are as necessary for you to understand even the rudimentary laws of Being, as courses in your colleges;

and guessed-at spirit knowledge from your bounded view must always fail in accurate wording."

It will be perceived that the answers to these questions are, from the beginning, evasive; but the real idea entertained clearly shines through the thin veil drawn over to conceal it. The questions pertain to the source, or authorship, of the "laws of spiritual life;" and this would generally be understood to be God. But on a technicality the spirits refuse to answer. The question is made plainer, and the answer is that "spirits are not bondaged by *persons*;" that is to say that spirits have nothing to do with personalities, and that no personal being has anything to do with those laws. There is therefore no God who formulates and promulgates them. No wonder the question followed, how they came to know these laws; and it was a very convenient answer that we will know when we get there [pg 082] and have lost all physical perceptions. A desire for some explanation of those laws is met with the not very satisfactory information that they (the spirits) would have to give those in our sphere a course of teaching, like a college course, before we could understand even the rudimentary laws of Being. The only thing clear in all this is that there is no God; at least no personal God such as the Bible reveals. To the "grand whole," whatever that may be, they give the name of the "All of Being." In answer to a question concerning "personalities," they are called "atoms emanating from the same source—parts of the great All of Being, partaking of the general characteristics of the grand whole."—*Page 149*.

Reader, how does all this compare in your own mind with the God of the Bible, the Creator of all things, the loving Father of us all, who has for his creatures more tender regard and pity than a father can feel for his own children, whose very name and nature is Love, and who has purposed infinite good for all men, and will carry it out unless they, as free moral agents, by their own sin, prevent his doing for them what he desires to do? The Bible is not responsible for the aspersions cast upon God by a false theology, which misrepresent his character and give occasion for the charges of vindictiveness and vengeance and awful tyranny, so freely made by fallen angels and wicked men. They do not belong to him who is the source of all goodness and mercy; and we would labor to bring those who have perverted views of God back to a right conception of [pg 083] the great Friend of sinners, as he has revealed himself in his holy word.

2. *They Deny Jesus Christ.*—Christ is revealed as the divine Son of the Father; and to deny that he was or is any more than any other man is surely to deny him; and the scripture says that "whosoever denieth the Son, the same hath not the Father." 1 John 2:23. The following is what the "spirits" began to teach in the earliest stages of Spiritualism concerning Christ:—

> "What is the meaning of the word Christ?—'Tis not, as generally supposed, the Son of the Creator of all things. Any just and perfect being is Christ. The crucifixion of Christ is nothing more than the crucifixion of the spirit, which all have to contend with before becoming perfect and righteous. The miraculous conception of Christ is merely a fabulous tale."—*Spiritual Telegraph, No. 37.*

How fully does this declaration that any good man is Christ open the way for the fulfilment of the Saviour's prophecy that in the last days many false Christs and false prophets shall arise, and shall deceive many. See Matt. 24:24. A prospectus of the *Truth Seeker* contained these words: "It shall be the organ through which the christs of the last dispensation will choose to speak."

A little later, July 19, 1862, there was published in the *Banner of Light* a lecture on Spiritualism by Mrs. C. L. V. Hatch, in which she spoke of Christ as follows:—

> "Of Jesus of Nazareth, personally, we have but little to say. Certain it is, we find sufficient that is divine in his life and teachings, without professing to believe in the fables of [pg 084] theologians respecting his birth and parentage. We are content to take the simple record as it stands, and to regard him as the son of Joseph and Mary, endowed with such purity and harmony of character as fitted him to be the Apostle and Revelator of the highest wisdom ever taught to man. It is the fundamental article in the creed of modern Christianity, that Jesus was divine in his nature, and of miraculous origin and nativity. Now, no human being of ordinary intelligence, unwarped by educational bias, would ever profess to believe in such a monstrous figment, which only shows the blindness of superstitious prejudice."

Here is something twenty-four years later. A séance reported in the *Banner of Light*, Oct. 9, 1886, gives the following questions and answer:—

> "*Ques.*—Do 'spirits' generally believe in the divinity of Jesus Christ; that he was the Son of God; that he was crucified, dead, and buried, and rose again the third day for the saving of all who should believe in him?
>
> "*Ans.*—No; spirits generally—advanced spirits, those who are intelligent, having studied deeply into the principles of life—do not accept the theory of the divinity of Jesus Christ; they do not believe that he was crucified for mankind, in the accepted understanding of that term."

Some years ago a class was formed in New York City for the purpose of investigating what is called the spiritual philosophy. Before that class, Dr. Weisse said:—

> "Friend Orton seems to make rather light of the communications from spirits concerning Christ. It seems, nevertheless, that all the testimony received from advanced spirits only shows that Christ was a medium and reformer in Judea; that he now is an advanced spirit in the sixth sphere; but that he never claimed to be God, and does not at present. I have had two communications to that effect. I have also read some that Dr. Hare had. If I am wrong in my views of the Bible, I should like to know it, for the spirits and mediums *do not contradict me.*"

[pg 085]
The peculiar insult here purposely offered to the Saviour will be appreciated when it is noted that at about the same time the spirits located Thomas Paine, the well-known skeptic, in the seventh sphere, one sphere above that of Christ. He must therefore have progressed very rapidly, seeing he so quickly surpassed Christ, who had over 1700 years the start of him.

Before the same class Dr. Hare is reported to have spoken as follows, which we give without assuming any responsibility for the spiritual grammar therein exhibited:—

> "He said that he had been thus protected from deception by the spirits of Washington and Franklin, and that they had brought Jesus Christ to him, with

> whom he had also communicated. He had first repelled him as an impostor; but became convinced afterward that it was really him. He related that he had learned from that high and holy spirit, that he was not the character that Christendom had represented him to be, and not responsible for the errors connected with his name, but that he was, while on earth, a medium of high and extraordinary powers, and that it was solely through his mediumistic capabilities that he attained so great knowledge, and was enabled to practice such apparent wonders."

When Christ was upon earth, it was envy, jealousy, and malice that moved the Pharisees against him (Matt 27:18); and it seems that he is followed by the same feelings in the spirit world. This is natural; for he who fired the hearts of the Pharisees with their malignant spirit, is the same one, as we have seen, who is working through the powers of darkness in the unseen world to-day. Any way to degrade Christ in the minds of men to a level with, [pg 086] or below, the mediums of our time, and make it appear that they can do as great wonders as he, seems to be the object in view.

There is plainly manifest an irrepressible desire on the part of spirits and mediums to show Christ to be inferior to the leaders of other great religions of the world, as Buddha, Confucius, Zoroaster, etc. Thus, at a seance held in 1864 (*Banner of Light*, June 4), the spirits were questioned as follows:—

> "*Ques.*—Have you ever seen Confucius or Zoroaster?
>
> "*Ans.*—Yes, many times.
>
> "*Q.*—In the order of degree, which stands the higher in moral excellence—Jesus Christ, Confucius, or Zoroaster?
>
> "*A.*—Confucius stands in morality higher than the other two.... Jesus himself claims to have been inspired to a large extent, by this same Confucius. And if we are to place reliance upon the records concerning each individual, we shall find that Jesus spoke the truth when he tells us that he was inspired by Confucius."

Indeed! Where are the records referred to? Where and when did Jesus "speak" the words attributed to him? And where does he tell *us*, that he was inspired by Confucius? So we are to believe, are we, that the gospel of Jesus Christ, is only a rehash of what was originally wrought out in the brain of Confucius, and not words fresh from the fountain of light given him by his Father in heaven, to speak, as he claimed them to be? Yet he was a high and *holy* medium. We wonder what standard of holiness and perfection the spirits can have.

But still later, in 1896, we find the spirits putting forth the same teaching in reference to Jesus Christ. In "Automatic, or Spirit Writing," pp. 148, 149, we have this:—

[pg 087]

"*Ques.*—Do you accept Jesus as the model of spiritual knowledge?

"*Ans.*—Shall you give us a better example?

"*Q.*—Well, we are willing to accept him as one of many, but not as chief.

"*A.*—Change the name. Call him by other names—Buddha, Krishna, or Mohammed, the spirit is one—is ever and ever the same. Spirit is one, not many, however often the name is changed.

"*Q.*—Were not Jesus, Buddha, and Mohammed distinct personalities?

"*A.*—No more than all atoms emanating from the same source—parts of the great All of Being, partaking of the general characteristics of the grand whole—but yielding to environments, showed marked individualism, such as the force of the times in which they appeared would create in their characters.

"*Q.*—Are these leaders of religious thought not distinct individualities now?

"*A.*—No, not on spiritual planes, which do not recognize any now."

Thus they persist in denying that Jesus holds any pre-eminent position as a religious teacher. He may as well be called Buddha, Krishna, or

Mohammed as Jesus. They are all the same spirit, all atoms of the great "All of Being," all as much alike as three drops of water from the same ocean, and what is more bewildering still, they have now all lost their individuality in the spirit world. How, then, can it be told that Christ is in the sixth sphere, and Paine in the seventh? Such teachers, though they may claim to be good spirits, are branded as antichrist by both John and Jude. John says: "Who is a liar but he that denieth that Jesus is the Christ? He is antichrist that denieth the Father and the Son." 1 John 2:22. Again, "Every spirit that confesseth not that Jesus Christ is come in the flesh is not of [pg 088] God." 1 John 4:3. According to the spirits, Jesus Christ has no more come in the flesh than have Buddha, Mohammed, Confucius, Zoroaster, or any other religious teacher. They all simply yielded to their environments, and showed marked individualism while on this earth, and have now become absorbed in the "great whole" in the spirit world. Thus, as Jude says (verse 4), they deny "the only Lord God, and our Lord Jesus Christ."

So much for their denial of Christ in his person. They also deny him in his offices; for to deny and ridicule what he came to do, is one of the most effectual ways of denying him. The great work of Christ was the shedding of his blood to atone for the sins of the world; and the spirits are particularly bitter in denouncing that idea. If such sentiments were uttered only by open and professed scoffers, it would not do so much harm; but it is not unusual to find those bearing the title of "Reverend" descanting on these themes in a manner to show themselves antichrist, according to the definition of that term by John. And even this need not surprise us; for the sure word of prophecy has foretold that some who have once held the true faith will depart therefrom to give heed to seducing spirits, and doctrines of devils. 1 Tim. 4:1.

One R. P. Wilson, to whose name is attached the ministerial title, in his lectures on "Spiritual Science," said:—

> "Although as a believer in true spiritual philosophy, we cannot receive the orthodox views of salvation, yet we recognize [pg 089] the birth of a Saviour and Redeemer into the universal hearts of humanity, *wherein truly the deity is incarnate*, dwelling in the interior of man's spirit. We believe that each soul of man is born with his or her Saviour within them; for as man is an embodiment of the universe in epitome, he contains in his central nature

an incarnation of deity. The germ of immortal unfoldings resides within the spirit of it, which needs only appropriate conditions to call forth the expanding and elevating powers of the soul."

In "Spiritual Science Demonstrated," p. 229, Dr. Hare said:—

"Since my spirit sister's translation to the spheres, she has risen from the fifth to the sixth sphere. It has been alleged by her that her ascent was retarded by her belief in the atonement."

A "spirit" calling himself Deacon John Norton, as reported in the *Banner of Light*, said:—

"I used to believe in the atonement; I honestly believed that Christ died to save the world, and that by and through his death all must be saved if saved at all. Now I see that this is folly—it cannot be so. The light through Christ, the Holy One, shone in darkness; the darkness could not comprehend it; and thus it crucified the body, and Christ died a martyr. He was not called in that way, that by the shedding of his blood, the vast multitude coming after him should find salvation. Everything in nature proves this false. They tell me here that Christ was the most perfect man of his time. I am told here also that he is worthy to be worshiped, because of his goodness; and where man finds goodness he may worship. God's face is seen in the violet, and man may well worship this tiny flower."

In the pantheism of Spiritualism, every object in nature, the tiny flower, the pebbles, the trees, the birds and bees, are worthy to be worshiped as much as Christ. In one breath the spirits extol him as a most perfect man, pre-eminent in goodness and [pg 090] worthy to be worshiped, and in the next, place him in a position which would make him the greatest fraud and impostor that ever lived. Such inconsistencies show that Christ is a miracle which evil men and evil angels know not how to dispose of.

As they deny Christ, they must, logically, deny the doctrine of his second coming. This doctrine is made of especial importance and prominence in the New Testament. The nature of that coming, its manner, and the circumstances attending it are so fully described, that no one who adopts the Bible view can possibly be deceived by false christs. But the church and the world have been turned away from the true doctrine of the second advent, and the way is thus prepared for the great deceptions of the last days. Spiritualism is one of these, and claims that it is itself that second coming. Joel Tiffany, a former celebrated teacher of Spiritualism, has said:—

> "I must look for the coming of my Lord in my own affection. He must come in the clouds of my spiritual heavens, or he cannot come for any benefit to me."

And through Mrs. Conant, a famous medium of the early days of Spiritualism, the controlling spirit said:—

> "This second coming of Christ means simply the second coming of truths that are not themselves new, that have always existed.... He said, 'When I come again, I shall not be known to you.' Spiritualism is that second coming of Christ."—*Banner of Light, Nov. 18, 1865.*

But the Bible description of this event is, the revelation of the Lord himself in the clouds of [pg 091] heaven in the glory of the Father, the reverberating shout of triumph, the voice of the archangel, the trump of God, the flash of his presence like that of the lightning, the wailing of the tribes of the earth, as they thus behold him, while unprepared to meet him, and the resurrection of the righteous dead. And where and when have these inseparable accompaniments of that event been seen? They do not occur when a person is converted from sin, nor do they occur in the dying chamber, nor have they occurred in Spiritualism; and until they do take place, the second coming of Christ is not accomplished.

Many seek to dispose of such testimony as this, by making it all figurative, or meeting it with a bold denial, as in the case of the resurrection of the body. And the way has been too well prepared for this condition of things, by much of the teaching of popular orthodoxy, which turns the early records of the Bible into childish allegory, perverts the true doctrine of the coming and kingdom of Christ, and denies the resurrection of the dead, by destroying its necessity through the immortality of the soul. On the vital point of the resurrection, Dr. Clarke makes this noteworthy remark:—

> "One remark I cannot help making,—The doctrine of the resurrection appears to have been thought of much more consequence among the primitive Christians than it is *now*! How is this?—The apostles were continually insisting on it, and exciting the followers of God to diligence, obedience, and cheerfulness through it. And their successors in the present day seldom mention it! So the apostles preached, and so the primitive Christians believed; so we preach and so our hearers [pg 092] believe. There is not a doctrine in the gospel on which more stress is laid; and there is not a doctrine in the present system of preaching which is treated with more neglect."—*On 1 Corinthians 15* (*original edition*).[3]

In view of the way the Bible has been treated by its professed friends, it is no wonder that infidelity prevails, and Spiritualism prospers.

3. *They Deny the Bible.*—The denial of God and Christ, as set forth above is, of course, a denial of the Bible; and not much need therefore be added on this point. We quote only a few representative utterances. Doctor Hare ("Spiritual Science Demonstrated," p. 209) says:—

> "The Old Testament does not impart a knowledge of immortality, without which religion were worthless. The notions derived from the gospels are vague, disgusting, inaccurate, and difficult to believe."

As to the Old Testament, it would seem doubtful whether Mr. Hare ever read far enough to find (1) Job exclaiming: "For I know that my Redeemer liveth, and that he shall stand at the latter day upon the earth: and though after my skin worms destroy this body, yet in my flesh shall I see God: whom I shall see for myself, and mine eyes shall behold, and not another; though my reins be consumed within me" (or, as the margin reads: "My reins within me are consumed with earnest desire [for that day];") or (2) David: "I shall be satisfied, when I awake, with [pg 093] thy likeness;" or (3) Isaiah: "Thy dead men shall live, together with my dead body shall they arise. Awake and sing, ye that dwell in the dust;" or (4) Ezekiel: "Behold, O my people, I will open your graves, and cause you to come up out of your graves;" or (5) Daniel: "Many of them that sleep in the dust of the earth shall awake, some to everlasting life, and some to shame and everlasting contempt;" and (6) Hosea: "I will ransom them from the power of the grave, I will redeem them from death." Job 19:25-27; Ps. 17:15; Isa. 26:19;

Eze. 37:12; Dan. 12:2; Hosea 13:14. And as for the New Testament, it is no doubt "disgusting" to many Spiritualists to read that "the fearful, and unbelieving, and the abominable, and murderers, and whoremongers, and sorcerers, and idolaters, and all liars, shall have their part in the lake which burneth with fire and brimstone: which is the second death;" and that without the city "are dogs, and sorcerers, and whoremongers, and murderers, and idolaters, and whosoever loveth and maketh a lie." Rev. 21:8; 22:15.

Communications from spirits are offered in place of the Bible as a better source of instruction, the Bible being denounced, as above quoted, as "vague, inaccurate, and difficult to believe." A brief comparison of the two will furnish pertinent evidence on this point. Take, on the Bible side, for example, a portion of the record of creation (Gen. 1:1-5):—

> "In the beginning God created the heaven and the earth. And the earth was without form, and void; and darkness was [pg 094] upon the face of the deep. And the Spirit of God moved upon the face of the waters. And God said, Let there be light: and there was light. And God saw the light, that it was good: and God divided the light from the darkness. And God called the light Day, and the darkness he called Night. And the evening and the morning were the first day."

The facts stated in this record, the profoundest minds can never comprehend; the language in which they are expressed, a little child can understand. The statements are plain and simple, a perfect model of perspicuous narrative. Place by the side of this an account of the same event, as given us from the "spheres." The spirits have undertaken to produce a new Bible, beginning, like the old, with the creation; and this is the way it starts out, through the mediumship of "Rev." T. L. Harris:—

> "1. In the beginning God, the Life in God, the Lord in God, the Holy Procedure, inhabited the dome, which, burning in magnificence primeval, and revolving in prismatic and undulatory spiral, appeared, and was the pavilion of the Spirit: In glory inexhaustible and inconceivable, in movement spherical, unfolded in harmonious procedure disclosive.

"2. And God said, Let good be manifest! and good unfolded and moral-mental germs, ovariums of heavens, descended from the Procedure. And the dome of disclosive magnificence was heaven, and the expanded glory beneath was the germ of creation. And the divine Procedure inbreathed upon the disclosure, and the disclosure became the universe."

We will inflict no more of this "undulatory spiral" nonsense on the reader. He now has both records before him, and can judge for himself which is the more worthy of his regard. There have been Spiritualists who, writing in their normal state, and not yet fully divorced from the influence of their [pg 095] former education, have acknowledged the authenticity of the Bible, and the doctrines of Jesus as recorded in the gospels. But these, it is claimed, are to be understood according to a spiritual meaning which underlies the letter; and this spiritual meaning generally turns out to be contrary to the letter, which is a virtual denial of the record itself. But the quotations here given (only a specimen of the multitudes that might be presented) are given on the authority of the "spirits," whose teachings are what we wish to ascertain.

They Deny All Distinction Between Right And Wrong.

There is implanted in the hearts of men by nature, a sense of right and a sense of wrong. Even those who know not God, nor Christ, nor the gospel, possess this power of discrimination. This is what Paul, in Rom. 2:15, calls "the work of the law written in their hearts, their conscience also bearing witness, and their thoughts the meanwhile accusing or else excusing one another." That this distinction should now be denied by a class in a civilized community, professing to be advanced thinkers and teachers, among whom are found the learned, the refined, and the professedly pious, shows that we have fallen upon strange times. To be sure, many of them talk fluently of the beauty and perfection of divine laws; but in the sense in which they would have them understood, they rob them of all characteristics of law. The first great essential of law is [pg 096] authority; but this they take away from it; the next is penalty for its violation; but this they deny, and thus degrade the law to a mere piece of advice. The "Healing of the Nations," an authoritative work among Spiritualists, pp. 163, 164, says:—

> "Thus thy body needs no laws, having been in its creation supplied with all that could be necessary for its government. Thy spirit is above all laws, and above all essences which flow therein. God created thy spirit from within his own, and surely the Creator of law is above it; the Creator of essences must be above all essence created. And if thou hast what may be or might be termed laws, they are always subservient to thy spirit. Good men need no laws, and laws will do bad or ignorant men no good. If a man be above law, he should never be governed by it. If he be below, what good can dead, dry words do him?

> "True knowledge removeth all laws from power by placing the spirit of man above it."

A correspondent of the *Telegraph* said of this work, "The Healing of the Nations:"—

> "According to its teaching, no place is found in the universe for divine wrath and vengeance. All are alike and forever the object of God's love, pity, and tender care—the difference between the two extremes of human character on earth, being as a mere atom when compared with perfect wisdom."

This is a favorite comparison with them,—that the difference between God and the best of men is so much greater than the extremes of character among men,—the most upright and the most wicked,—that the latter is a mere atom, and not accounted of in God's sight. That there is an infinite difference between God and the best of men, is all true; for God is infinite in all his attributes, and man is very imperfect at the best. But to argue from this that [pg 097] God is inferior to man, so that he cannot discern difference in character here, even as man can plainly discern it, seems but mad-house reasoning. What would we think of the man who had the same regard for the thief as for the honest man, for the murderer as for the philanthropist? To ignore such distinctions as even men are able to discern would destroy the stability of all human governments; what then would be the effect on the divine government? God has given his law—holy, just, and good—to men, and commanded obedience. He has attached the penalty to disobedience: "The soul that sinneth, it shall die," "The wages of sin is death." Eze. 18:20; Rom. 6:23. And in the judgment, the distinction God makes in character will be plainly declared; for he will set the righteous on his right hand, but the wicked on the left. Matt. 25:32, 33.

This view of the failure of law, and the absence of all human accountability, naturally leads to a bold denial of sin and the existence of crime. The "Healing of the Nations," p. 169, says: "Unto God there is no error; all is comparatively good." The same work says that God views error as "undeveloped good." A. J. Davis ("Nature of Divine Revelation," p. 521) says: "Sin, indeed, in the common acceptation of that term, does not really exist."

A discourse from J. S. Loveland, once a minister, reported in the *Banner of Light*, contained this paragraph:—

[pg 098]

"With God there is no crime; with man there is. Crime does not displease God, but it does man. God is in the darkest crime, as in the highest possible holiness. He is equally pleased in either case. Both harmonize equally with his attributes—they are only different sides of the same Deity."

In "Automatic Writing" (1896), p. 139, a question was asked concerning evil, meaning sin and crimes among men. The spirit answered that these were conditions of progress, and were so necessary to elevation that they were to be welcomed, not hated. The questions and answers are as follows:—

"*Ques.*—Can you give us any information in regard to the so-called Devil—once so firmly believed in?

"*Ans.*—Devil is a word used to conjure with.

"*Q.*—Well, then, as the word itself doubtless arose from the word 'evil,' which means to us unhappiness, can you give us an explanation of the existence of evil?

"*A.*—Evil—as you who are the greatest sufferers from it, name one of the conditions of progress—is as necessary, aye, more so, than what you call good, to your and our elevation to higher spheres. It is not to be hated, but welcomed. It is the winnowing of the grain from the chaff. Children of truth, don't worry over what to you seems evil; soon you will be of us and will understand, and be rejoiced that what you call evil persists and works as leaven in the great work of mind versus matter.

"*Q.*—But it seems to us impossible that brutal crimes like murder, assassinations, or great catastrophes, by which the innocent are made to suffer at the hands of malicious and cruel persons, should work for ultimate good?

"*A.*—Percipients of the grand whole of Being can understand but may not state to those on your plane, the underlying good making itself asserted even through such dreadful manifestations of human imperfections as the crimes you name.

"When asked why certain wrongs were allowed to be perpetuated, this answer was given:—

[pg 099]

"There is a law of psychical essence which makes necessary all these ephemeral entanglements which to you seem so severe, and you will yet see from your own standpoint of reason why such hardships must be endured by questioning souls on the highway of progress.

"*Q.*—But do you from your vantage ground of larger knowledge grow careless that such injustice is done?

"*A.*—We do care, but cannot remedy.

"*Q.*—Why can't you remedy?

"*A.*—Because humanity is but an embryo of existence.

"*Q.*—If you can perceive the trials and sorrows of mortals, and can interfere to save them, why do you not more often do so?

"*A.*—When undeveloped souls pay the price of development, we stand aloof, and let the play go on. Interference will do no good."

In view of such a confession, what becomes of the many claims put forth by other spirits that they are ever hovering near their friends to assist and guard them, to help and inspire them, and keep them from evil and danger? These say that those terrible crimes (and this would include all crimes) are all necessary, that they are tending to develop souls, and bring them to higher spheres, and thus are just as laudable as good actions; so they settle back in a gleeful mood, and "let the play go on;" let wicked men cultivate and develop and practice their evil propensities, and the innocent suffer. Well may men pray to be delivered from such a spirit assembly as that.

In "Healing of the Nations," p. 402, Dr. Hare says:—

> "That anything should, even for an instant, be contrary to his will, is inconsistent with his foresight and omnipotency. [pg 100] It would be a miracle that anything counter to his will should exist."

A lecture on the "Philosophy of Reform," given by A. J. Davis, in New York City, bears testimony to the same effect:—

> "In the Hebrew and Christian Scriptures, it is affirmed that sin is the transgression of the law. But by an examination of nature, the true and only Bible, it will be seen that this statement is erroneous. It gives a wrong idea of both man and law.... It will be found impossible for man to transgress a law of God."

Thus they very illogically assume that if God has the will or the power to prevent evil, it could not exist, and therefore, if there is such a God, he is responsible, forgetting that God is long-suffering, and bears long with vessels of wrath fitted for destruction, before they pass beyond the limits of his mercy and perish. But Mr. Davis says further:—

> "Reformers need to understand that war is as natural to one stage of human development as peace is natural to another. My brother has the spirit of revenge. Shall I call him a demon? Is not his spirit natural to his condition? War is not evil or repulsive except to a man of peace. Who made the non-resistant? Polygamy is as natural to one stage of development as oranges are natural to the South. Shall I grow indignant, and because I am a monogamist, condemn my kinsman of yore? Who made him? Who made me? We both came up under the confluence of social and political circumstances; and we both represent our conditions and our teachers. The doctrine of blame and praise is natural only to an unphilosophical condition of mind. The spirit of complaint—of attributing 'evil' to this and that plane of society—is natural; but is natural only to undeveloped minds. It is a profanation—a sort of atheism of which I would not be guilty."

[pg 101]
The Bible says, "Woe unto them that call evil good, and good evil; that put darkness for light and light for darkness." Isa. 5:20. And it makes another declaration which finds abundant confirmation in the sentiments quoted above: "Because sentence against an evil work is not executed speedily,

therefore the heart of the sons of men is fully set in them to do evil." Eccl. 8:11.

Having thus attempted to destroy in the minds of men all distinction between good and evil, all being alike in God's sight, and all equally good, they try to make the way a little broader and easier for men to give full rein to all the propensities and inclinations of an evil heart, by teaching that there is no Lawgiver and Judge before whom men must appear to give an account of their deeds, but that they are responsible to themselves alone, and must give account only to their own natures. Thus Hon. J. B. Hall, in a lecture reported in the *Banner of Light*, Feb. 6, 1864, said:—

> "I believe that man is amenable to no law not written upon his own nature, no matter by whom given.... By his own nature he must be tried—by his own acts he must stand or fall. True, man must give an account to God for all his deeds; but how?—Solely by giving account to his own nature—to himself."

At a séance reported in the *Banner of Light*, May 28, 1864, the following question was proposed, and the answer was by the communicating spirit:—

> "*Ques.*—To whom or to what is the soul accountable?

> "*Ans.*—To no Deity outside the realm of its own being, certainly; to no God which is a creation of fancy; to no [pg 102] Deity who dwells in a far-off heaven, and sits upon a white throne; to no Jesus of Nazareth; to no patron saint; to no personality; to no principle outside our own individual selves."

The "Healing of the Nations," p. 74, says:—

> "Man is his own saviour, his own redeemer. He is his own judge—in his own scales weighed."

A little over twenty years after the birth of Spiritualism, Aug. 25, 1868, the Fifth National Convention of Spiritualists was held in Corinthian hall, Rochester, N. Y., at which a formal "Declaration of Principles" was set forth. From the seventh and eighth paragraphs, under principle 20, we quote the following:—

> "*Seventh*, To stimulate the mind to the largest investigation ... that we may be qualified to *judge for ourselves* what is right and true. *Eighth*, To deliver from *all bondage to authority*, whether vested in *creed*, *book*, or *church*, except that of received truth."

This is the same principle of man's responsibility to no one but himself, authoritatively adopted. What a picture have we now before us! Destroy man's belief in, and reverence for, God and Christ, as they do; lead him to ridicule the atonement, the only remedy for sin; make him disbelieve the Bible; take away from his mind all distinction between right and wrong, and assure him that he is accountable to no one but himself; and how better could one prepare the way to turn men into demons. All this the spirits, by their teaching, seek to do. And can any one fail to foresee the result? Comparatively a small proportion of the inhabitants of this country [pg 103] have committed themselves to these views; consequently but little of the legitimate fruit as yet appears; but take human nature as it is and suppose all the inhabitants of this land to act on these principles, and then what would we have?—A pandemonium, a scene of anarchy, riot, bloodshed, and all depths of rottenness and corruption—in short, a hell so much worse than that to which the Devil is popularly assigned, that he would at once change his location and here take up his abode.

That this statement is none too strong, will appear as we look a moment at some of the results which have already developed themselves among the friends of such views, and as their inevitable fruit. The tendency can by no possibility be otherwise than to atheism and all immorality. As has been already remarked, the repulsive features were made much more prominent in the early stages of Spiritualism than at the present time. They are now held in the background. The literature touching these points has been remodeled, and an air of respectability and religion assumed. Most of the quotations therefore date some years back, and would be charitably withheld were there any evidence of reform either present or prospective. But where or when have these principles ever been officially repudiated, and evidence given that the consequent practices had been abandoned? That there are many Spiritualists of upright and moral lives, and honorable members of society, in the best sense of that term, we gladly believe; but is not this because they are living above [pg 104] their principles; and due, not to the influence, but rather to the non-influence of real Spiritualism upon their lives? The quotations given are from those who have been prominent among Spiritualists as authors and speakers. If they overdraw the picture, the responsibility is with them. Dr. B. P. Randolph, author of a work "Dealings with the Dead," was eight years a medium, then renounced Spiritualism long enough to expose its character, then returned to it again, unable to break entirely away from the spell it has fastened upon him. He gives his opinion of it in the following scathing words:—

> "I enter the arena as the champion of common sense, against what in my soul I believe to be the most tremendous enemy of God, morals, and religion, that ever found foothold on the earth;—the most seductive, hence the most dangerous, form of sensualism that ever cursed a nation, age, or people. I was a medium about eight years, during which time I made three thousand speeches, and traveled over several different countries, proclaiming its new gospel. I now regret that so much excellent breath was wasted, and that my health of mind and body was well nigh ruined. I have only begun to regain both since I totally abandoned it, and to-day had rather see the cholera in my house, than be a spiritual medium.

> "As a trance speaker, I became widely known; and now aver that during the entire eight years of my mediumship, I firmly and sacredly confess that I had not the control of my own mind, as I now have, one twentieth of the time; and before man and high heaven I most solemnly declare that I do not now believe that during the whole eight years, I was sane for thirty-six consecutive hours, in consequence of the trance and the susceptibility thereto.

> "For seven years I held daily intercourse with what purported to be my mother's spirit. I am now fully persuaded that it was nothing but an evil spirit, an infernal demon, [pg 105] who, in that guise, gained my soul's confidence, and led me to the very brink of ruin. We read in Scripture of demoniac possession, as well as abnormal spiritual action. Both facts exist, provable to-day; I am positive the former does. A. J. Davis and his clique of Harmonialists say there are no evil spirits. I emphatically deny the statement. Five of my friends destroyed themselves, and I attempted it, by direct spiritual influences. Every crime in the calendar has been committed by mortal movers of viewless beings. Adultery, fornication, suicides, desertions, unjust divorces, prostitution, abortion, insanity, are not evils, I suppose. I charge all these to this scientific Spiritualism. It has also broken up families, squandered fortunes, tempted and destroyed the weak. It has banished peace

from happy families, separated husbands and wives, and shattered the intellect of thousands."

The following is an extract from the writings of J. F. Whitney, editor of the New York *Pathfinder*. His view of the subject accords with that of Dr. Randolph:—

"Now, after a long and constant watchfulness, seeing for months and for years its progress and its practical workings upon its devotees, its believers, and its mediums, we are compelled to speak our honest conviction, which is, that the manifestations coming through the acknowledged mediums, who are designated as rapping, tipping, writing, and entranced mediums, have a baneful influence upon believers, and create discord and confusion; that the generality of these teachings inculcate false ideas, approve of selfish individual acts, and endorse theories and principles, which, when carried out, debase and make men little better than the brute. These are among the fruits of Modern Spiritualism, and we do not hesitate to say that we believe if these manifestations are continued to be received, and to be as little understood as they are, and have been since they made their appearance at Rochester, and mortals are to be deceived by their false, fascinating, and snakelike charming powers, which go with them, the day will come when the world will require the appearance of [pg 106] another Saviour to redeem the world from its departing from Christ's warnings.... Seeing, as we have, the gradual progress it makes with its believers, particularly its mediums, from lives of morality to those of sensuality and immorality, gradually and cautiously undermining the foundation of good principles, we look back with amazement to the radical change which a few months will bring about in individuals; for its tendency is to approve and endorse each individual act and character, however good or bad these acts may be....

"We desire to send forth our warning voice, and if our humble position as the head of a public journal, our known advocacy of Spiritualism, our experience, and the conspicuous part we have played among its believers, the honesty and the fearlessness with which we have defended the subject, will weigh anything in our favor, we desire that our opinions may be received, and those who are moving passively down the rushing rapids to destruction should pause, ere it be too late, and save themselves from the blasting influence which those manifestations are causing."

Every one who knows anything about Spiritualism has heard of Cora Hatch, who traveled extensively, and manifested her powers as an extemporaneous lecturer before astonished multitudes. One of her husbands, Dr. Hatch, renounced Spiritualism, and the following is from the testimony he bore concerning it:—

> "The most damning iniquities are everywhere perpetrated in spiritual circles, a very small percentage of which ever comes to public attention. I care not whether it be spiritual or mundane, the facts exist, and should demand the attention and condemnation of an intelligent community.... The abrogation of marriage, bigamy, accompanied by robbery, theft, rape, are all chargeable upon Spiritualism. I most solemnly affirm that I do not believe that there has, during the last five hundred years, arisen any people who are guilty of so great a variety of crimes and indecencies as the Spiritualists of America.

[pg 107]

> "For a long time I was swallowed up in its whirlpool of excitement, and comparatively paid but little attention to its evils, believing that much good might result from the opening of the avenues of Spiritual intercourse. But during the past eight months I have devoted my attention to critical investigation of its moral, social, and religious bearing, and I stand appalled before the revelations of its awful and damning realities."

Much testimony of this nature might be given from those who have had similar experiences and equally favorable facilities for judging of the character of Spiritualism. We present only a few extracts more.

Dr. Wm. B. Potter of New York, in an article under the head of "Astounding Facts," and also in a tract entitled, "Spiritualism as It Is," gives the result of his experience and observations. His testimony is the more valuable, since he writes not from the standpoint of one who has renounced Spiritualism, whose feelings may for the time be overwrought, and his language stronger than would be used in calmer moments. When he wrote, he was still an advocate of Spiritualism, and spoke as a friend who would, if possible, induce Spiritualists to reform their faith and their manner of living. He says:—

> "Fifteen years of critical study of Spiritual literature, an extensive acquaintance with the leading Spiritualists, and a patient, systematic, and thorough examination of the manifestations for many years, enable us to speak from actual knowledge, definitely and positively, of 'Spiritualism as It

Is.' Spiritual literature is full of the most insidious and seductive doctrines, calculated to undermine the very foundations of morality and virtue, and lead to the most unbridled licentiousness.

[pg 108]

"We are told that 'we must have charity,' that it is wrong to blame any one, that we must not expose iniquity, as 'it will harden the guilty,' that 'none should be punished,' that 'man is a machine, and not to blame for his conduct,' that 'there is no high, no low, no good, no bad,' that 'sin is a lesser degree of righteousness,' that 'nothing we can do can injure the soul or retard its progress,' that 'those who act the worst will progress the fastest,' that 'lying is right, slavery is right, murder is right, adultery is right,' that 'whatever is, is right.'

"Hardly can you find a Spiritualist book, paper, lecture, or communication that does not contain some of these pernicious doctrines; in disguise, if not openly. Hundreds of families have been broken up, and many affectionate wives deserted by 'affinity-seeking' husbands. Many once devoted wives have been seduced, and left their husbands and tender, helpless children, to follow some 'higher attraction.' Many well-disposed but simple-minded girls have been deluded by 'affinity' notions, and led off by 'affinity hunters,' to be deserted in a few months, with blasted reputations, or led to deeds still more dark and criminal, to hide their shame."

The same writer also mentions a fact which shows where the responsibility of all this looseness of morals belongs. He says:—

"At the National Spiritual Convention at Chicago, called to consider the question of a national organization, the only plan approved by the committee, especially provided that no charge should ever be entertained against any member, and that any person, without any regard to his or her moral character, might become a member."

The fact that no plan could find approval which did not provide that they should never be blamed nor called to account for any of their deeds, shows on what points they felt the most anxious, and plainly proves that they belong to the class of which Christ spoke, who loved darkness rather than light, [pg 109] and who would not come to the light lest their deeds should be reproved. John 3:19-21.

It is unpleasant to wade through pools of filth, and we therefore spare the reader quotations from those Spiritualists who have not only avowed the most revolting practices of free love, but openly advocated the same, and endeavored to induce others to come out likewise, on the ground that they were only honestly and publicly admitting what the others believed and practiced in secret. For the same reason we pass by the notorious Woodhull and Claflin, and Hull and Jamieson episodes, in this field, which, in the illustration and language of another, "burst upon the country like a rotten egg three thousand miles in diameter!"

It may be said that these things are in the past and the situation has now greatly changed. For the benefit of those who thus flatter themselves we introduce one more quotation. It is from "The Law of Psychic Phenomena," by T. J. Hudson (A. C. McClurg & Co., Chicago, 1894). The language is candid and conciliatory, and the author cannot be accused of any undue prejudice on the question of which he speaks. On page 335, he says:—

> "I do not charge Spiritualists as a class with being advocates of the doctrines of free love. On the contrary, I am aware that, as a class, they hold the marriage relation in sacred regard. I cannot forget, however, that but a few years ago some of their leading advocates and mediums proclaimed the doctrine of free love in all its hideous deformity from every platform in the land. Nor do I fail to remember that the better class of Spiritualists everywhere repudiated the [pg 110] doctrine, and denounced its advocates and exemplars. Nevertheless the moral virus took effect here and there all over the country, and it is doing its deadly work in secret in many an otherwise happy home. And *I charge a large and constantly growing class of professional mediums with being the leading propagandists* of the doctrine of *free love*. They infest every community in the land, and it is well known to all men and women who are dissatisfied or unhappy in their marriage relations, that they can always find sympathy by consulting the average medium, and can, moreover, find justification for illicit love by invoking the spirits of the dead through such mediums."

We have italicized that passage in the foregoing which shows that the deadly evil is still working in secret, and that a large and constantly growing number of professionals are aiding and abetting the iniquity.

Dangers Of Mediumship.

A few testimonies will show that when one gives himself or herself up to the control of the spirits, such ones take a most perilous position. The spirits insist on their victims becoming passive, ceasing to resist, and yielding their whole wills to them. Some of their persuasive words are these: "Come in confidence to us;" "Let our teachings deeply impress you;" "You must not doubt what we say;" "Learn of us;" "Obey our directions and you will be benefited;" "Seek to obtain knowledge of us;" "Have faith in us;" "Fear not to obey;" "Obey us and you will be greatly blessed;" etc., etc. Mesmerists operate in the same way. They gain control of their subjects in the same way that the spirits mesmerize their mediums, and when under [pg 111] their control, the spirits cause them to see whatever they bring before them, and hear according to their wills, and do as they bid. And the things they suppose they see and hear, and what they are to do, are only such things as exist in the mind of the mesmerizing power. The subject is completely at the mercy of the invisible agency; and to put one's self there is a most heaven-daring and hazardous act. Mr. Hudson ("Law of Psychic Phenomena," p. 336) says:—

> "To the young whose characters are not formed, and to those whose notions of morality are loose, the dangers of mediumship are *appalling*."

To further gain the confidence of mortals, the spirits claim to be the ones who answer their prayers. In "Automatic Writing," p. 142, we have this:—

> "*Ques.*—Will our friends tell us whether from their point of view, there is any real efficacy in prayer?

> "*Ans.* [by spirits].—Shall not 'a soul's sincere desire' arouse in discarnate and free spirits effort to make that sincere desire a reality? What good can come from aspirations on mortal planes, save through the efforts to make those aspirations realized on spiritual planes, by the will of freed spirits?"

Mediums are unable to resist the powers of the unseen world when once under their control. Professor Brittan ("Telegraphic Answer to Mahan," p. 10), concerning mediumship, says:—

> "We may further add in this connection that the trance mediums for spirit intercourse are equally irresponsible. Many of them are totally unable to resist the powers which come to them from the invisible and unknown realms."

[pg 112]
Dr. Randolph ("Dealings with the Dead," p. 150) shows the dangers of mediumship, as follows:—

> "I saw that one great cause of the moral looseness of thousands of sensitive-nerved people on earth, resulted from the infernal possessions and obsessions of their persons by delegations from those realms of darkness and (to all but themselves) unmitigated horror. A sensitive man or woman—no matter how virtuously inclined—may, unless by constant prayer and watchfulness they prevent it and keep the will active and the sphere entire, be led into the most abominable practices and habits."

This same writer, in the same work, pp. 108, 109, says:—

> "Those ill-meaning ones who live just beyond the threshold, often obtain their ends by subtly infusing a semi-sense of volitional power into the minds of their intended victims, so that at last they come to believe themselves to be self-acting, when in fact they are the merest shuttlecocks bandied about between the battledores of knavish devils on one side, and devilish knaves upon the other, and between the two the poor fallen wretches are nearly heart-reft and destroyed."

A work by A. J. Davis called "The Diakka, and their Earthly Victims," mentions the nature of these denizens of the spirit world, and their wonderful location. The country (to speak after the manner of men) which they inhabit, is so large that it would require not less than 1,803,026 diameters of the earth to span its longitudinal extent. This he had from a spirit he calls James Victor Wilson, a profound mathematician! This space is occupied by spirits who have passed from earth, who are "morally deficient, and affectionally unclean."—*Page* [pg 113] *7.* The same spirit, Wilson, describes the diakka as those "who take insane delight in playing parts, in juggling tricks, in personating opposite characters to whom prayers and profane utterances are of equi-value; surcharged with a passion for lyrical narrations; one whose every attitude is instinct with the schemes of specious reasoning, sophistry, pride, pleasure, wit, subtle convivialities; a boundless disbeliever, one who thinks that all private life will end in the all-consuming self-love of God."—*Page 13.* On page 13 he says further of them, that they are "never resting, never satisfied with life, often amusing themselves with jugglery and tricky witticisms, invariably victimizing others; secretly tormenting mediums, causing them to exaggerate in speech, and to falsify in acts; unlocking and unbolting the street doors of your bosom and memory; pointing your feet into wrong paths, and far more."

What this "far more" is, we are left to conjecture. The advertisement of this book says that it is "an explanation of much that is false and repulsive in Spiritualism." W. F. Jamieson, in a Spiritualist paper, called these diakka "a troop of devils," and quoted Judge Carter as saying: "There is one thing clear, that these diakka, or fantastic or mixed spirits, are very numerous and abundant, and take any and every opportunity of obtruding themselves."

Hudson Tuttle, author of "Life in Two Spheres" and other Spiritualistic works, speaks of "a communication, through a noted medium, to Gerald [pg 114] Massey from his 'dog Pip,' the said Pip 'licking the slate and writing with a good degree of intelligence.' " He adds, "Mr. Davis would say that 'Pip' was a 'diakka,' and to-morrow he will communicate as George Washington, Theodore Parker, or Balaam's ass. This diakka is flesh, fish, or fowl, as you may desire."

Some idea of how the spirits sometimes torment the mediums, as hinted at above, may be gained from the following instance. In "Astounding Facts from the Spirit World," pp. 253, 254, Dr. Gridley describes the case of a medium sixty years of age, living near him in Southampton, Mass. The sufferings inflicted upon him "in two months at the hands of evil spirits would fill a volume of five hundred pages." Of these sufferings, the following are specimens:—

> "They forbade his eating, to the very point of starvation. He was a perfect skeleton; they compelled him to walk day and night, with intermissions, to be sure, as their avowed object was to torment him as much and as long as possible. They swore by everything sacred and profane, that they would knock his brains out, always accompanying their threats with blows on the forehead or temples, like that of a mallet in the hands of a powerful man, with this difference, however; the latter would have made him unconscious, while in full consciousness he now endured the indescribable agony of those heavy and oft-repeated blows; they declared they would skin him alive; that he must go to New York and be dissected by inches, all of which he fully believed. They declared that they would bore holes into his brain, when he instantly felt the action suited to the word, as though a dozen augers were being turned at once into his very skull; this done, they would fill his brain with bugs and worms to eat it out, when their gnawing would instantly commence. [pg 115] These spirits would pinch and pound him, twitch him up and throw him down, yell and blaspheme, and use the most obscene language that mortals can conceive; they would declare that they were Christ in one breath, and devils in the next; they would tie him head to foot for a long time together in a most excruciating posture; declare they would wring his neck off because he doubted or refused obedience."

Who can doubt that such spirits are the angels of the evil one himself? Dr. Gridley in the same work, p. 19, gives the experience of another medium, for the truthfulness of which he offers the fullest proof:—

> "We have seen the medium evidently possessed by Irishmen and Dutchmen of the lowest grade—heard him repeat Joshua's drunken prayers [Joshua was a strong but brutish man he had known in life], exactly like the original,— imitate his drunkenness in word and deed—try to repeat, or rather act over his most brutal deeds (from which for decency's sake, he was instantly restrained by extraordinary exertion and severe rebuke)—snap and grate his teeth most furiously, strike and swear, while his eyes flashed like the fires of an orthodox perdition. We have heard him hiss, and seen him writhe his body like the serpent when crawling, and dart out his tongue, and play it exactly like that reptile. These exhibitions were intermingled with the most wrangling and horrible convulsions."

These descriptions, it would seem, ought to be enough to strike terror to any heart at the thought of being a medium. But there is yet another phase of the subject that should not be passed by. These fallen spirits who are engineering the work of Spiritualism, to maintain their "assumed characters," and "play their parts" like the aforesaid diakka, represent that disembodied spirits "just over the threshold," still retain the characteristics they bore in life, such [pg 116] as a disposition to sensuality and licentiousness, love of rum, tobacco, and other vices, and that they can, by causing the medium to plunge excessively into these things, thereby still gratify their own propensities to indulge in them. The following sketch by Hudson Tuttle, a very popular author among Spiritualists, is somewhat lengthy, but the idea could not better be presented than by giving it entire. In "Life in Two Spheres," pp. 35-37, he says:—

"Reader, have you ever entered the respectable saloon? Have you ever watched the stupid stare of the inebriate when the eye grew less and less lustrous, slowly closing, the muscles relaxing, and the victim of appetite sinking over on the floor in beastly drunkenness? Oh, how dense the fumes of mingled tobacco and alcohol! Oh, what misery confined in those walls! If you have witnessed such scenes, then we need describe no further. If you have not, then you had not better hear the tale of woe. Imagine to yourselves a bar-room with all its sots, and their number multiplied indefinitely, while conscience-seared and bloated fiends stand behind the bar, from whence they deal out death and damnation, and the picture is complete. *One has just arrived from earth.* He is yet uninitiated in the mysteries and miseries of those which, like hungry lions, await him. He died while intoxicated—was frozen while lying in the gutter, and consequently is attracted toward this society. He possessed a good intellect, but it was shattered beyond repair by his debauches.

" 'Ye ar' a fresh one, aint ye?' coarsely queried a sot, just then particularly communicative.

" 'Why, yes, I have just died, as they call it, and 'taint so bad a change after all; only I suppose there'll be dry times here for the want of something stimulant.'

" 'Not so dry; lots of that all the time, and jolly times too.'

" 'Drink! Can you drink, then?'

" 'Yes, we just can, and feel as nice as you please. But all can't, not unless they find one on earth just like them. [pg 117] You go to earth, and mix with your chums; and when you find one whose thoughts you can read, he's your man. Form a connection with him, and when he gets to feeling *good*, you'll feel so too.—There, do you understand me? I always tell all fresh ones the glorious news, for how they would suffer if it wasn't for this blessed thing.'

" 'I'll try, no mistake.'

" 'Here's a covey,' spoke an ulcerous-looking being; 'he's of our stripe. Tim, did you hear what an infernal scrape I got into last night? No, you didn't. Well, I went to our friend Fred's; he didn't want to drink when I found him; his dimes looked so extremely large. Well, I *destroyed that feeling*, and made him think he was dry. He drank, and drank, more than I wanted him to, until I was so drunk that I could not break my connection with him, or control his mind. He undertook to go home, fell into the snow, and came near freezing to death. I suffered awfully, ten times as much as when I died.'... Reader, we draw the curtain over scenes like these, such as are daily occurring in this society."

In these cases the whole evil of the indulgences of course falls upon the mediums; and who would wish to assume personal relation with such a world, and be forced to bear in their own bodies the evils of the unhallowed indulgences of unseen spirits, against their will?

Other scenes represented as taking place in the spirit land, are most grotesque and silly and would be taken as a burlesque upon Spiritualism, were they not put forth in all gravity by the friends and advocates of that so-called new revelation. Thus Judge Edmunds, giving an account of what he had seen in the spirit world, mentions the case of an old woman busy churning, who promised him, if he would call again, a drink of buttermilk; he speaks [pg 118] of men fighting, of courtezans trying to continue their lewd conduct; of a mischievous boy who split a dog's tail open, and put a stick in it, just to witness its misery; of the owner of the dog, who, attracted by its cries, discovered the cause, and beat the boy, who fled, but was pursued and beaten and kicked far up the road. See Edmund's "Spiritualism," Vol. II, pp. 135-144, 181, 182, 186, 189. Surely here are the diakka playing their pranks in all their glory.

Miscellaneous Teaching.

On the leading points of faith as held by Christians generally, quotations have been given to show sufficiently what the spirits teach, and the object they are trying to effect. But the reader will be interested to learn what they teach on some other points which incidentally appear in their communications.

Spiritualists object most strenuously to the idea of unconsciousness in death, or to the Bible declaration, "The dead know not anything." But the spirits themselves teach this very thing. Thus Judge Edmunds, Vol. II, Appendix B, p. 524, quotes the confession of a spirit that he was totally unconscious for a time, he could not tell how long, and awoke to consciousness gradually; and that the state of unconsciousness differs with different persons, depending on circumstances. A. J. Davis admits that Professor Webster was eight days and a half unconscious.—*"Death and the After Life," pp. 18, 19.*

[pg 119]
Through Mrs. Conant, medium, in *Banner of Light*, June 3, 1865, we have this information: "It is said that some spirits require a thousand years to awake to consciousness. Is this true?—Yes, this is true." In "Automatic Writing," p. 93, the spirits teach the same thing to-day. If others deny such statements, it only shows that their testimony is contradictory and therefore unreliable.

Again, the Bible doctrine that the incorrigibly wicked must cease from conscious existence, is denounced by Spiritualists; but on this point the spirits confess also:—

> "*Ques.*—Do I understand you to say that a diakka is one who believes in ultimate annihilation?
>
> "*Ans.*—Only yesterday one said to a lady medium, signing himself 'Swedenborg,' this: 'Whatsoever is, has been, will be, or may be, *that* I AM,

and private life is but the aggregative phantasms of thinking throblets rushing in their rising onward to the central heart of eternal death.'—*"Diakka"* p. 11.

"*Q.*—Does every human being continue life on higher planes?

"*A.*—Shall not all who are abortions die?"

"*Q.*—Do you mean that some born on this plane may spiritually die from lack of force to persist?

"*A.*—Yes—both women and men are born into the divine humanity who must necessarily perish, because they have not sufficient soul strength to persist."—*"Automatic Writing,"* pp. 101, 102.

There is, it seems, a purgatory in the spirit world. In answer to a question, a spirit replied:—

"There is a sphere in spirit life allotted to those who leave the earthly plane in spiritual ignorance, which is *not pleasing* to dwell upon, yet which is absolutely necessary to spiritual soul growth."—*Id., p. 90.*

[pg 120]
Spiritualism is claimed to settle the question of immortality; but the spirits confess themselves ignorant of it:—

"*Ques.*—On your plane do you arrive at certainty in regard to immortality?

"*Ans.*—We here are as *ignorant as you are* as to the ultimate of existence. Immortality is still an *undetermined issue*. One life at a time seems as pertinent with us as with you."—*Id., p. 103.*

The spirits' heaven, it seems, is not so desirable a place that it prevents their being homesick.

"*Ques.*—Why are you homesick?

"*Ans.*—Have not found out the real reason; things are so different from former ideas."—*Id., p. 111.*

Spirits are not allowed to tell too much about their condition, as the following question and answer show:—

"*Ques.*—Can't you tell us what makes it pleasanter,—describe so we can understand?

"*Ans.*—You'll find out as I did—*'gainst the rules here to tell....* Just be patient—it's all easy enough when you learn how. I was puzzled, but it all seems straight enough now."—*Id., p. 115.*

They teach the pre-existence of souls, and the old pagan doctrines of the reincarnation of souls, and the final absorption of all into Nirvana. A spirit having answered that all had been asserted in some other form, questions and answers followed from which we quote:—

"*Q.*—Is that statement an intimation of the truth of reincarnation?

"*A.*—Souls of all who have preceded you are centered in you in spite of your childish protests. Ask not of those [pg 121] predecessors; for they yet live in you, and you in them.... Long ago you and I went over the ground under eminent names.... Were not we together when Socrates and Aspasia talked?"—*Id., pp. 151, 152.*

"*Q.*—Can you tell us, at least, whether spirit, as a whole or in its individual atoms, exists eternally?

"*A.*—Yes; spirit as a whole is eternal—exists—did exist—by force of Powers you cannot understand. But you as individual, self-conscious, atomistic particles of spirit wholeness, are not eternal, and must return to the Primal Source."—*Id., p. 133.*

Spirits Cannot Be Identified.

Having now sufficiently examined the teaching of the spirits, a final question arises in regard to them, whether it is possible to identify them, and determine with any absolute certainty whether they are the spirits of the particular individuals they claim to be, or even spirits of the dead at all, or not. It should be distinctly borne in mind, always, that evil angels, whose existence has been proved from the Bible, whose nature and delight is to deceive, can walk the earth unseen, imitate and personate any individual, and reveal their characteristics of thought, writing, acts, form, and features, and make so perfect a counterfeit as to defy detection. How, then, can it be told what spirit it is, even though it shows the face and features of some well-known friend? On this topic, as on preceding questions, Spiritualists themselves may produce the evidence. President Mahan ("Discussion with Tiffany and Rhen," p. 13) remarks:—

> "Certain experiments have been made, in order to determine whether spirits are present. Individuals go in as [pg 122] inquirers, and get definite answers—in the first place, from *departed spirits* of persons *yet living*; in the second place, from departed spirits of persons who *never existed* here or anywhere else; in the third place, from the departed spirits of brute beasts."

When it is considered, as already noted, that spirits do their work through mesmeric power, it is easy to understand how the medium is made to believe that such and such a spirit is communicating when it is not so at all. This question of identity came up in the very early stages of Spiritualism, and is no nearer settled, on their own confession, now than then. A Mr. Hobart, in 1856, who claimed to be the first Spiritualist in Michigan, made the following admission:—

> "The spirit sometimes *assumes* the name of an individual belonging to the same church, to induce them to hear. This is necessary with some who are so bigoted they would not believe unless a name was assumed which they respected."

An article in the *Spiritual Telegraph*, of July 11, 1857, begins as follows:—

> "The question is continually being asked, especially by novitiates in spiritual investigations, How shall we know that the spirits who communicate with us are really the ones whom they purport to be?... In giving the results of our own experience and observation upon this subject, we would premise that spirits unquestionably can, and often do, personate other spirits, and that, too, often with such perfection as, for the time being, to defy every effort to detect the deception.... If direct tests are demanded at all, we would recommend that they be asked for the purpose of proving that the manifesting influence is that of *a spirit*, rather than to prove what *particular* spirit is the agent of its production."

[pg 123]
This is an entire begging of the whole matter in question; for it is not denied that it is *a* spirit; we want to know what *particular* spirit it is; but for that we must not ask; for it cannot be ascertained. The same article states that other and lower spirits often crowd in and take the place of the spirit communicating, without the knowledge of the medium. We might also quote "Spiritualism as It Is," p. 14, that "not one per cent. of the manifestations have had a higher origin than the first and second spheres, which are filled with low, ignorant, deceptive, mischievous, selfish, egotistical spirits;" and "Dealings with the Dead," p. 225, that "the fact is, good spirits do not appear one tenth as often as imagined."

Jan. 7, 1888, the following appeared in the *Banner of Light*:—

> "*Ques.*—What is the cause of our receiving inconsistent and untruthful communications? Does the blame, if any there is, rest with us or the controlling intelligence?

> "*Ans.*—There are spirits who delight in imposing upon mortals; they realize their power outside of material things, and that those who seek knowledge from them *cannot see nor get hold of them*; therefore to an extent they exercise a certain power over those mortals who approach; and if the mortals are themselves tricky by nature, insincere, ready to take advantage of others, whether it be at the time of sitting or in their daily life, rest assured they may be imposed upon by spirits from the other side who occupy a like plane of existence with themselves."

Mediums themselves will not trust the spirits, according to statements made as late as 1896. Mrs. S. A. Underwood, medium, in "Automatic Writing," p. 55, says:—

[pg 124]

> "With all my experience in it, I would not to-day venture upon any change, business venture, friendship, or line of conduct, advised from this source, unless my own common material sense endorsed it. Indeed, I would not take as fact any of its even reasonable advice without question, because it is not reliable as a guide in earthly affairs."

Spirit communication, then, certainly does not amount to much as a heavenly instructor, a celestial guide to enlighten the ignorance of men. Whatever we know ourselves, we may rely upon; all else is uncertain. Again, on p. 56, she says:—

> "Then the assumption of great names by apparently common-place minds is a very strange thing. I was horrified and annoyed when this occurred under my own hand, because that is one of the things which disgusted me with spiritual messages before this writing came to me, as I had occasionally glanced over such messages. When I protested against such assumption, I was told that 'Elaine and Guinevere' were not real beings, but types. So somewhere in our sphere are spirits who embody cleverness in creations of their own fancy, and adopt names suited to that fancy."

Thus the spirits themselves confess that the names they often assume are not those of real beings, but typical and fanciful. Nothing more, it would seem, is necessary to complete the condemnation of Spiritualism, so far as its own nature is concerned. When in addition to all else, it appears that the spirits cannot be identified; that the whole underlying claim that the spirits are the spirits of the dead, must itself be assumed; and that, too, in the face of the numberless known falsehoods and deceptions that are constantly issuing from the unseen realm,—there is nothing left for it to stand upon.

[pg 125]

Chapter Six.

Its Promises: How Fulfilled.

It is fair to call Spiritualism to account as to the fulfilment of the promises involved in its challenge to the world when it stepped upon the stage of action. No movement ever opened with more magnificent promises. It posed before the world as an angel of heavenly light. It claimed to be the second coming of Christ. It claimed to have been sent to regenerate mankind, and renovate the world. We give herewith a few of its spirit-inspired pretensions. Its "Declaration of Principles," Article 20, says:—

> "The hearty and intelligent convictions of these truths [the teachings of spirits] tend to energize the soul in all that is good and elevating, and to restrain from all that is evil and impure, ... to quicken all philanthropic impulses, stimulating to enlightened and unselfish labors for universal good."

In behalf of the cause of woman it says:—

> "Spiritualism has done more for the advancement of true womanhood than the Church or any of its accessories."—*Dr. Watson, in Banner of Light, April 16, 1887.*

Miss A. L. Lull, in the *Religio-Philosophical Journal* of Jan. 23, 1886, said:—

> "Spiritualism is the saviour of humanity, because it is reaching out toward the criminal, and in its effort to lift [pg 126] humanity to a higher plane, it is laying the foundation for future generations.... Spiritualism comes to cleanse out the dregs and wretchedness of humanity."

Mrs. Cora L. V. Richmond, in a mediumistic discourse reported in the *Banner of Light*, April 3, 1886, said:—

> "The Great Reformer of the world is Spiritualism.... When modern Spiritualism made its appearance, it said in so many words, I come to reform the world.... Spiritualism came to put the ax at the root of the tree of human evil, it came to decide upon the most important and vital thing connected with existence; *i. e.*, Is man only an evanescent, material, earthly being, or is he immortal?... Spiritualism came to reform death, to resolve it into life; came to reform fear, to resolve it into trust and knowledge; came to reform the darkness which rests upon humanity concerning the nature of man's existence."

In the same paper, April 6, 1887, was given the following prediction of the future of Spiritualism:—

> "Modern Spiritualism will grow, and deepen, and broaden, and strengthen, until all false creeds and dogmas shall be swept from the earth—when faith shall be buried in knowledge, when war shall be known no more, when universal brotherhood shall prevail to bless mankind."

In "Nineteenth Century Miracles," p. 79, M. Jaubert speaks as follows:—

> "Affirm to your people that man never dies, that his immortality is proved, not by books but by material and tangible facts, of which every one can convince himself; that anon our houses of correction, and our prisons, will disappear; suicide will be erased from our mortuary tables; and nobly borne, the calamities of earth shall no longer produce madness."

[pg 127]
Mrs. R. S. Lillie, in a speech at the Thirty-eighth Anniversary services in Horticultural Hall, Boston, Mass., and reported in the *Banner of Light*, of April, 1886, said:—

> "Christianity never had a Pentecost to be compared with modern Spiritualism. The latter is as far in advance of the former, as the electric light is in advance of the tallow dip of the past; for it is nineteen centuries ahead of it."

These are most astounding claims; and if there is any truth in them, Spiritualism ought to have shown itself as a great uplifting moral power, provided it has been able to get any foothold among the people. We therefore inquire what its success has been. On this point Professor Keck, at the Thirty-ninth Anniversary of Modern Spiritualism, at Bridgeport, Conn. (*Banner of Light*, April 9, 1887), said:—

> "It [Spiritualism] has made converts of more scientific men and profound thinkers than any other sect in the world. In thirty-nine years it has grown to ten or fifteen millions of believers, with thousands of mediums, a literature printed in every known language, and converts in every quarter of the globe."

With all these facilities and all this success, it surely has been able to make good its claims, and fulfil its promises, if its nature is such as it assumes, and its promises are good for anything; and its course should be marked by a great decrease of crime, by the promotion of virtue and a general improvement in the moral tone of society, wherever it has gone. For nearly fifty years it has now been operating in the world; and with all its glowing [pg 128] professions of what it was able to do, and its millions of converts, "energized to all that is good and elevating," its impress for good should everywhere be seen.

But what are the facts?—Just the reverse of what has been promised. Free love, which is free lust, has followed in its wake; homes have been ruined, families scattered, characters blighted; while insanity and suicide have been the fate, or the last resort, of too many of its victims. And outside of its own ranks, in the world at large, the fifty years since the advent of Spiritualism have been years of increase of crime and every evil in a fast growing ratio. Liquor drinking, tobacco using, gambling, prostitution, defalcations, robberies, bribery, municipal corruption, divorces, thefts, insanity, suicide, and murder, have increased in far more rapid ratio than the population itself.

The reader will remember the testimony of Dr. Randolph, p. 105, that five of his friends destroyed themselves, and he attempted it for himself, by direct spirit influences. The Philadelphia *Record*, of Feb. 17, 1894, speaks of the suicide of May Brooklyn in San Francisco, Cal.:—

> "The letters and papers left by the dead woman show plainly that in her grief over the death of Lovecraft she had dabbled in Spiritualism, and had finally reached the conclusion that her only chance of happiness lay in joining her lover in the other world."

A few figures, as samples, will be given just to emphasize the general statements. The following is from the Chicago *Tribune* of Jan. 1, 1893:—

> "The number of persons who have committed suicide in the United States during the year (1892), as gathered from telegraph and mail report to the *Tribune*, is 3860, as compared with 3331 last year (1891), 2640 in 1890, and 2224 in 1889. The total is much larger than that of any of the eleven preceding years."

The *Christian Reformer* gives the following figures of murders, suicides, and embezzlements from 1891-1893:—

> "Murders in 1893, 6615; increase over 1891 of 709.

> "Suicides in 1893, 4436; increase over 1892, 576; 1891, 1105.

> "Funds embezzled in 1893, $19,929,692; increase of 100 per cent. over 1892."

It may be asked, What has this to do with Spiritualism?—It is a test of the value of its promises. Spiritualism has been posing for fifty years as the "world's reformer," the great energizing, uplifting force to elevate mankind, the mighty power which has come to empty our workhouses and prisons, abolish suicides and all crime, the "electric light" compared with the "tallow dip" of the gospel. And yet with all these claims, with its millions of adherents, and the funds and influence at its command, it is allowing, year by year, crime to increase much faster than the population. Now if Spiritualism was the purifying, renovating power which it claims to be, such results could not have been seen. It is very evident, that, as a power in the world in behalf of righteousness and humanity, it has been of no account; and as between the forces of good and evil, its weight has been on the side of evil instead of good. It is thus that the author of [pg 130] Spiritualism, the father of deception, fulfils the promises made through that channel to deceive mankind. What organized, aggressive efforts against evil has Spiritualism ever shown? Where are its schools and colleges? Where are its hospitals and benevolent institutions? Where are its organized charities? and what are its millions of members doing to relieve suffering and distress, and turn men to better ways of living? The very aspect it presents to the world to-day, stamps the brand of Cain upon its brow. The Boston *Herald* of Dec. 17, 1874, said:—

> "Let Spiritualism produce some idea, utter some word, or perform some deed, which will have novelty, and yet be of manifest value to the human race, and it will make good its claims to our serious consideration. But it has not done this. For nearly thirty years it has been before the world in its present shape, and in all that time, with all its asserted command of earthly and superterrestrial knowledge, it has never done an act, or breathed a syllable, or supplied an idea which had any value as a contribution to the welfare of the race, or to its stock of knowledge. Its messages from learned men who are dead, have been the silliest bosh; its stories about life upon the planets are wretched guesses, many of which can be proved false by the astronomer; its visions have frightened scores of people into madhouses, and made semi-lunatics of hundreds of others."

If this charge was good as late as 1874, it is equally so at the present time. And thus are we forced to the conclusion that Spiritualism, judged by the light of its fair promises, is one of the most lamentable of delusions, and most stupendous of failures.

[pg 131]

Chapter Seven.

Spiritualism A Subject Of Prophecy.

We come now to one of the most timely and important features of this whole subject; for God in his word has foretold and forewarned the world of the movement here passing under review. He has made known the time when it should appear, the character it would bear, and the work it is to do. He has also connected this with the great event of all-overshadowing importance to this world, of which it is a startling sign and sure precursor; namely, the second coming of our Lord Jesus Christ. We ask the special attention of the reader to this part of the subject.

A word of digression may be allowed as to the place which prophecy holds in the word of God. Prophecy is that feature of the sacred volume which constitutes it a lamp to our feet and a light to our path. Ps. 119:105; 2 Peter 1:19. It is that which enables that word to be a guide to the hosts of Israel through the weary journey and the gloomy shades of time, giving to every era its "present truth," and showing the progress of the slow-revolving ages toward the great consummation. It [pg 132] is the golden credential which the Bible holds up to the world of its genuineness and authenticity.

Prophecy is peculiar to the Christian Scriptures. No other so-called sacred books contain this feature. It is not found in the Vedas, Shasters, or Puranas of the Hindus, nor the Zend Avestas of the Parsees, nor the Kojiki Nohonki, of the Shintos of Japan, nor the law books of Manu, nor the Koran of the Mohammedans, nor the Kan-Ying-Peen or Tao-Te-King of the Chinese, nor the Tripitakas of the Buddhists. The reason is obvious. Neither the minds of men nor of angels, either good or bad, can read the future. Divine omniscience alone can see the end from the beginning and foretell the great events that shall mark the history of the world, and affect the interests of the church. It is this that stamps the Bible as divine, and lifts it immeasurably above all other books. It is indeed passing strange that all cannot see this. Instead of being a book that grows obsolete and out of date with the passing years, like the productions of men, it is the only book ever seen upon the earth which is ever abreast of the times in every age, and lifts the veil of the future before him who honestly and reverently seeks its pages for a knowledge of the truth. Those who ignore or despise the prophecies, rob the Bible of one of the brightest stars in its crown of glory.

To be entitled to claim credit as divine, any book or system should be able to show that it can correctly foretell the future. The spirits see this, [pg 133] and, knowing that they cannot do it, discountenance and discourage all such efforts. Here is a little of their teaching on the subject:—

> "*Ques.*—Why are so many predictions made through mediums, which prove false?
>
> "*Ans.*—Wonderful *guesses* are sometimes made by daring spirits.
>
> "*Q.*—Can you tell us anything of the future?
>
> "*A.*—Pharos says you must not ask questions of the future—spirits who *prophesy* are *not good* spirits.
>
> "*Q.*—Do you mean that it is not best for us to know the future?
>
> "*A.*—Souls on your plane are undergoing discipline, and it would cost more than it is worth to foretell the future of your state."—"*Automatic Writing,*" *pp. 141, 142.*

Spiritualists rail at God for prohibiting from Adam and Eve, in the garden, the tree of the knowledge of good and evil, to keep them in ignorance. What will they say to these spirits who coolly answer that "it would cost more than it is worth" to give them any knowledge of future events? This, perhaps, they will consider all right because it isn't God who says it.

1. Let us then see what God has said of the time and work and significance of Spiritualism. Over seven hundred years before Christ, the prophet Isaiah wrote of our time, as follows: "And when they shall say unto you, Seek unto them that have familiar spirits, and unto wizards that peep and that mutter, should not a people seek unto their God? for the living to the dead? To the law and to the testimony; if they speak not according to this word, it is because there is no light in them."

[pg 134]
Here is certainly a prophecy that a time would come when just such a work as Spiritualism is now doing would be a distinguishing feature of the age. The present must be the time referred to, because it has never been so in any past age; and the present meets the specifications in every particular. It shows that the only safety for any one now is to seek unto his God, and make the law and the testimony, the word of God, the great standard by which to try all spirits. 1 John 4:1. And another great event is directly connected with this, that is, the second coming of Christ; for according to verses 16-18, the disciples are then looking for him.

2. Matt. 24:24: "For there shall arise false Christs, and false prophets, and shall show great signs and wonders; insomuch that, if it were possible, they shall deceive the very elect."

A deception of no ordinary power is here brought to view. It really results in the division of Christendom; for all but the elect are carried away by it. In its own claims, Spiritualism fulfils the "Christs" and "prophets" part of the declaration, claiming of course to be true, while the Bible says it is "false." The signs and wonders are beginning to be seen in the many "inexplicable" phenomena attending Spiritualism. But many more startling exhibitions, as will be presently shown, are yet to appear. We charge upon Spiritualism, so far, the fulfilment of this prophecy. But mark! this occurs when the Son of man is about to appear "as the lightning cometh out of the east, and shineth even unto the [pg 135] west" (verse 27); and it is one of the prominent signs of that event. See the prophecy from verse 23 to verse 35. Mark and Luke also dwell upon the same prediction, as gathered from the lips of our Lord himself.

3. Heb. 10:28, 29: "He that despised Moses' law died without mercy under two or three witnesses. Of how much sorer punishment, suppose ye, shall he be thought worthy, who hath trodden under foot the Son of God, and hath counted the blood of the covenant, wherewith he was sanctified, an unholy thing, and hath done despite unto the Spirit of grace?"

It is the bold stand which Spiritualism has taken against Christ and the atonement, that makes this scripture applicable to that work. The apostle is speaking of the times when the great "day is approaching" (verse 25); when it is but a little while, and he that shall come, will come and will not tarry (verse 37), and the introduction of verse 29, in such a connection, becomes a prophecy that such an outbreak against Christ and his atoning work would be seen when he is about to come again. And the fulfilment we are now beholding in Spiritualism.

4. Rev. 12:12: "Woe to the inhabiters of the earth and of the sea! for the devil is come down unto you, having great wrath, because he knoweth that he hath but a short time."

This scripture locates itself. It is when Satan knows that he has but a little time to work, and hence it must be in the last days. At this time he [pg 136] descends upon the world in an avalanche of wrath. "Wrath" is a misleading term. The words θυμόν μέγαν signify the strongest and most intense emotion of the mind. If the object is to accomplish some particular end, they would indicate the most intense, concentrated, energetic, and persistent efforts to that purpose, using every means, and bringing to bear every influence to reach the result in question. Satan, as we have seen, has an object in deceiving the human family, as far as possible, to their destruction, by signs and wonders. In this work, according to the prophecy before us, he will go to the extent of his power, and show his most potent signs. Bringing the supposed forms and features of the dead before living witnesses, is his most successful method at the present time. But as this work is, as yet, done largely in the dark, it gives more room for jugglery and imposition. The time will come, however, when, in open light, counterfeit materializations of the dead will swarm on earth, and deceive, if it were possible, the very elect—*i.e.*, all who cannot meet the deception with the potent weapon—"It is written, The dead know not anything, neither have they any more a

portion forever [in the present state of things] in anything that is done under the sun."

5. Rev. 13:13, 14: "And he doeth great wonders, so that he maketh fire come down from heaven on the earth in the sight of men, and deceiveth them that dwell on the earth by the means of those miracles which he had power to do."

This prophecy relates to some earthly government represented by a symbol with two horns like a lamb. [pg 137] Verse 11. It is part of a prophecy beginning with chapter twelve, and ending with verse 5 of chapter fourteen. It is not the place here to introduce an exposition of this prophecy. It is only necessary to state that the position taken is that the lamblike symbol represents our own government, the United States of America.[4] And the great wonders that he does, apply to the marvelous manifestations of Spiritualism. It is a significant fact that Spiritualism arose in this country, thus fitting itself exactly to the prophecy. The climax of the wonders brought to view in the text, making "fire come down from heaven on the earth in the sight of men," has not yet been reached. More is therefore to be developed. Yea, this wonder-working power is to go forward till that which, in the time of Elijah, was the test between the false god Baal and the Lord Jehovah, is brought to pass, and fire is made to come down from heaven on the earth in the sight of men. And the sad feature of this case will be that the multitudes, not perceiving the change of issue, will take the act down here to be a test of truth, as it was in the days of Elijah.

Taken in connection with other portions of the book of Revelation, this prophecy reveals clearly what the agency that works the miracles is. The dragon, representing paganism (Rev. 12:3, 4); the beast, representing the papacy (Rev. 13:1-10); and the lamblike symbol, representing Protestantism, [pg 138] or more specifically, Protestant America (Rev. 13:11-17), constitute the symbols of this prophecy. For convenience, let us designate them as *A*, *B*, and *C*; respectively. *C* works his miracles in sight of *B*; *B* and *C* are again brought to view in Rev. 19:20, and there *C* is called "the false prophet." We know the false prophet here is the same as *C*, because he works miracles before *B*, the same as *C* does in chapter 13:14. All together, *A*, *B*, and *C* are brought to view in Rev. 16:13, and unclean spirits like frogs are said to come out of their mouths; and then verse 14 tells what they are: "For they are spirits of devils, working miracles." This, then, not the spirits of dead men, is the agency that works the miracles of chapter 13:13, 14. We follow the subject so far, at this point, merely to identify the agency that works the miracles, and shall have more to say upon it. But before passing, we would remind the reader that here also the subject is connected with the second coming of Christ; for the prophecy of Revelation 13 ends with the redemption of the church which immediately follows. Rev. 14:1-5.

6. 2 Thess. 2:9-12: "Even him, whose coming is after the working of Satan, with all power and signs and lying wonders, and with all deceivableness of unrighteousness in them that perish; because they received not the love of the truth, that they might be saved. And for this cause God shall send them strong delusion, that they should believe a lie: that they all might be damned who believed not the truth, but had pleasure in unrighteousness."

[pg 139]
Here, again, we have the great fact brought out with still more startling emphasis, that there is to be a great outbreaking of Satanic power among men, just before and up to, the coming of Christ. And if we already see the preliminary and even far-advanced working of this power in Spiritualism, the world should stand aghast at the perils of the times in which we live. The coming of Christ is brought to view in verse 8, and verse 9 states that at that time Satan will be working with all power. The common version is calculated to obscure this passage. The words "even him" (verse 9) are wrongly and unnecessarily supplied. Literally rendered, the last clause of verse 8, and the first of verse 9 would read as follows: "Whom the Lord ... shall destroy with the brightness of his [Christ's] coming; of whom [Christ] the coming is, after [or at the time of] the working of Satan," etc. The word "after" is from, the Greek κατα (*kata*), which when referring to time, as in this case, does not mean "after or according to," but "within the range of, during, in the course of, at, about," as in 2 Tim. 4:1, where it is rendered "at."

So here is a plain declaration that at the very time when Christ comes Satan will be working in the hight of his power, by signs and lying wonders

(wonders to prove a lie) to keep the people under falsehood and deception. Verses 10-12 tell who his victims are, and why they become such: they are those who preferred the pleasures of sin to the practice of righteousness, and so would not receive the truth, [pg 140] nor the love of it. In all such cases God's throne is clear. He always, as in this case, sets truth first before the people, gives them a chance, and calls upon them to embrace it, and be saved. But when men, as free moral agents, whom God will not force into his kingdom, refuse to receive the truth, shut their eyes, close their ears, and steel their hearts against it, and find their pleasure in unrighteousness, in going in just the opposite direction;—what can God do for them? We leave the skeptic himself to answer. For more years than Spiritualism, in its present phase, has been before the world, several religious bodies have made a specialty of the great Bible truth concerning the state of the dead, and life only in Christ, which effectually shields all those who receive it against the rapping delusion.

7. Rev. 18:2: "And he cried mightily with a strong voice, saying, Babylon the great is fallen, is fallen, and is become the habitation of devils, and the hold of every foul spirit, and a cage of every unclean and hateful bird."

Among the many predictions given in the word of God touching the last days, is one which foretokens a wide-spread and lamentable declension in the religious world. The phrase which embodies it, is the one just quoted, "Babylon is fallen." The term "Babylon" is not intended nor used as a term of reproach, but rather as a descriptive word setting forth the very undesirable condition of "mixture" and "confusion" in the religious world. It is certainly not the Lord's will, who prayed that all his [pg 141] people should be one, that scores or hundreds of divisions and sects should exist within his church. That is owing, exclaims the Catholic, to the Protestant rule of private judgment. It is not. It is owing to that Pandora's box of mystical interpretation placed in the church by old Origen, that prince of mischief-makers. By this method, which has no method and no standard, the interpretations of God's word will ever be as various and numerous as the whims and fancies that may find a place in the minds of men.

But all this confusion must be remedied in that church which will be ready for the second advent; for no people will be prepared for translation but such as worship the Lord in both *spirit* and *truth*. To bring the church to this point, a call has been sent to Christendom in the special truths for this time. Most turn away, but some are taking the stand to which these circumstances summon them. The process is simple. It is but to read and obey God's word in the light of what is called the literal rule of interpretation. No other rule would ever have been thought of, if the Devil had let the minds of men alone. By this rule the true Sabbath would always have been maintained a perfect safeguard against idolatry in the earth; the law would have held its place as a perfect, immutable, and eternal rule of conduct, a safeguard against the antinomianism of all ages and the Spiritualism of to-day; the view that the dead remain unconscious in the grave till the resurrection, would always have [pg 142] been held, and then there could have been no purgatory, no masses for the dead, no Mariolatry, no saint worship—in short, no Roman Catholicism, and no Universalism, nor Spiritualism; the true nature of the coming and kingdom of Christ would not have been lost sight of, and the peace and safety fable of a temporal millennium never could have existed.

To say nothing of other errors that would be corrected, suppose all Christendom stood together on these four simple truths, how much division could there have been in the Christian world? A second denomination could not have existed. And what would have been the condition of things?—As different from the present condition as one can well imagine—no paganism, no Roman Catholicism, no Protestantism, no multiplied sects, no Spiritualism,—but Christianity, broad, united, free, and glorious. Some are taking their stand on these truths, and so will be shielded from the delusions of these last days, for which the way, by ages of superstition and error, has been so artfully prepared. Every one must stand upon them who is governed by the literal rule of interpretation; for they are read in so many words out of the sacred volume itself. But the churches generally reject them, often with bitterness, scorn, and contempt, and some even with persecution. And this is why Babylon has fallen.

That organization, called in Rev. 17:5: "Mystery, Babylon the Great, the Mother of Harlots and Abominations of the Earth," has been very generally applied by Protestants to the Roman Catholic [pg 143] Church; but if that church is the mother, who are the daughters? This question has been asked for many years. Alexander Campbell said:—

> "The worshiping establishments now in operation throughout Christendom, incased and cemented by their voluminous confessions of faith, and their ecclesiastical constitutions, are not churches of Jesus Christ, but the legitimate daughters of that mother of harlots—the Church of Rome."

Lorenzo Dow said:—

> "We read not only of Babylon, but of the whore of Babylon, styled the mother of harlots, which is supposed to mean the Romish church. If she be a mother, who are her daughters? It must be the corrupt national established churches that came out of her."

The great sin charged against Babylon, is unlawful connection with the kings of the earth. The church should be entirely free from the state. But now the churches of America, which have for long years borne so noble a part, are clamoring for a union with the state, calling for a recognition of God's name in the Constitution, and God's law in the courts, and that the government be run on Christian lines. Old, antiquated laws which they find upon the statute books of various States, they are beginning to use to persecute those who differ in belief with them; and they seek for the enactment of more stringent Sunday laws for the same purpose. And when they shall succeed in getting full control of the state, they will have severed the last link that has held them to their high estate, show themselves true members of the Babylonian family, [pg 144] and sink in spirit and practice to the level of the elder Rome.

Rev. 14:8 was fulfilled in 1844.[5] Since then the churches have been going down in spirituality and godliness, catering more and more to the world, indulging in carnal amusements, festivals, wife auctions, and kissing bees, to the very border line of decency, but especially filling up with the influences mentioned in Rev. 18:2, till the leaven of Spiritualism is fast penetrating the whole mass. Yet there are a multitude of God's people connected with these churches, who deplore the situation, and for whom a crisis is approaching. The cry is again to be raised, "Babylon is fallen, come out of her my people." We verily believe the time has come when that call should be made and heeded; for a little further progress in the evil path upon which we have entered, will surely provoke the just judgments of heaven. Verses 4, 5.

8. 2 Tim. 3:8: "Now as Jannes and Jambres withstood Moses, so do these also resist the truth: men of corrupt minds, reprobate concerning the faith."

The first five verses of this chapter portray a dark list of eighteen sins which will characterize professed Christians in the last days; for those who bear the characters described, have a *form of godliness*, but deny the power thereof. The three following verses plainly describe certain members of the spiritualistic [pg 145] fraternity; and they are said to be of the same sort. This prophecy therefore becomes parallel to that which has just been examined. The fall of Babylon prepares the popular churches for Spiritualism. Here the practice of these sins in the churches, makes them of the same sort with Spiritualists, so that they fraternize well together. Jannes and Jambres withstood Moses by the wonders they were able to perform; so these will resist the truth through the wonders of Spiritualism. And this is in the last days where we now are. So Babylon's fall just precedes the coming of Christ.

9. Rev. 16:14: "For they are the spirits of devils, working miracles, which go forth unto the kings of the earth and of the whole world, to gather them to the battle of that great day of God Almighty."

The work of the spirits reaches its climax in the scene here brought to view. Their last mission is to go to the kings of the earth to gather them to the battle of that great day of God Almighty. In this conflict, so far as this earth is concerned, the great controversy between Christ and Satan closes in the triumph of Him who rides forth on a white horse at the head of the white-horsed armies of heaven. The beast and false prophet are hurled into a lake of fire, and the remnant, the kings of the earth and their armies, are slain by the sword of him upon whose vesture is inscribed the all-conquering title, "King of kings and Lord of lords." Rev. 19:11-21.

[pg 146]

But before these spirits can thus influence the kings of the earth, they must make their way to them and bring them under their control. They have already shown great facility in this work, giving promise of what they will be able to do in the near future. A work by Hudson Tuttle, "What Is Spiritualism?" p. 6, names the following among the late and living crowned heads, nobility, etc., who have been supporters of Spiritualism:—

> "Emperor Alexander, of Russia; Louis Napoleon, of France; Queen Victoria, of England; Prince and Princess Metternich; Prince Wittgenstein, Lieutenant Aide-de-camp to the emperor of Russia; Hon. Alexander Axahof, Russian Imperial Councilor, St. Petersburg, Russia; Baron Guldenstuble, of Paris; Baron Von Schick, of Austria; Baron Von Dirkinck, of Holmfield, Holstein; Le Comte de Bullet, of Paris; Duke of Leuchtenberg, of Germany. Of England there are Lord Lyndhurst, Lord Lindsay, Lord Adare, Lord Dunraven, Sir W. Trevilyan, Countess Carthness, Sir T. Willshire, Lady Cowper, Sir Charles Napier, Sir Charles Isham, Bart., Colonel E. B. Wilbraham, of the English army," etc.

The late Alexander III, of Russia, and the queen of Spain are also reckoned among the number. Thus, so far as the agency of the spirits is concerned, there is nothing in the way of the speedy fulfilment of Rev. 16:14.

www.ingramcontent.com/pod-product-compliance
Lightning Source LLC
Chambersburg PA
CBHW081118080526
44587CB00021B/3648